IT HAPPENED ON CAPE COD

It Happened In Series

IT HAPPENED ON
CAPE COD

Shawnie M. Kelley

TWODOT®

GUILFORD, CONNECTICUT
HELENA, MONTANA
AN IMPRINT OF THE GLOBE PEQUOT PRESS

To buy books in quantity for corporate use
or incentives, call **(800) 962–0973, ext. 4551,**
or e-mail **premiums@GlobePequot.com.**

A · T W O D O T® · B O O K

Front cover: Pilot whales on beach. Library of Congress, LC-USZ62-113105
Back cover: Hauling in a cod aboard a dory. Library of Congress, LC-USW3-002175-E
Text design by Nancy Freeborn
Map by M. A. Dubé © Morris Book Publishing, LLC

Library of Congress Cataloging-in-Publication Data
Kelley, Shawnie M.
It happened on Cape Cod/Shawnie M. Kelley—1st ed.
    p. cm.—(It happened in)
  Includes bibliographical references and index.
  ISBN 0-7627-3824-3
    1. Cape Cod (Mass.)—History—Anecdotes. I. Title. II. It happened in series.
F72.C3K45 2006
—dc22

2005024923

Manufactured in the United States of America
First Edition/First Printing

To my mother
Bonnie "Kitty" Emery

CONTENTS

ACKNOWLEDGMENTS

I would like to thank my mother for reading every word of every story and offering encouragement and her honest opinion of each. My sister, Amanda Kelley, likewise contributed a good deal to the evolution of several stories. I would also like to acknowledge my fiancé and fellow Cape Cod explorer, Kevin Foy. His willingness to make detours and his patience while I researched this book during our personal time on the Cape is much appreciated.

A big thanks goes to all the nice people at the historical societies, visitor's centers, Cape Cod Community College, and Cape Cod National Seashore who took the time to respond to phone calls and e-mails, send out information and offer personal insight. Finally, thank *you* for purchasing *It Happened on Cape Cod*. I hope you enjoy reading this as much as I enjoyed writing it.

CAPE COD

INTRODUCTION

Cape Cod is the bared and bended arm of Massachu-
setts: the shoulder is at Buzzard's Bay; the elbow, or
crazy-bone is at Cape Mallebarre [Chatham]; the wrist
at Truro; and the sandy fist at Provincetown . . . box-
ing with northeast storms, and, ever and anon, heav-
ing her Atlantic adversary from the lap of the earth.

—HENRY DAVID THOREAU

DURING THE 1850S, HENRY DAVID THOREAU spent several weeks walk-
ing the "bared and bended arm of Massachusetts," taking in its
atmosphere and recording his thoughts. The imagery that fills
Thoreau's Cape Cod memoirs are the same images that come to
mind a century and a half later: sandy dunes covered with billowing
grass, tall ships sunken in icy nor'easters, and the Atlantic Ocean battering seaside shanties. He was visionary enough to recognize the
powerful appeal and thought-provoking nature of the Cape, and pre-
dicted this coast would be a place of resort for those who truly wished
to experience the seaside—and he was right.

Today, tourism is the Cape's number one industry, but Thoreau's
contagious reverence for solitude and natural history is not lost on
those of us living in the twenty-first century.

People continue to flock to Cape Cod in search of peace and quiet, history and folklore, shipwrecks and ghost stories. Some are fascinated with the Cape because of its colonial and maritime history, while others just come for the beaches. Whatever the reasons, nearly 400 years of European history fill every nook and cranny of every harbor and beach.

It Happened on Cape Cod is a collection of short stories that illustrate four centuries of perseverance, struggles, and successes. They are tales of people who have endured remarkable isolation, survived wars, weathered storms, and made and lost fortunes within a single generation. Legendary pilgrims and notorious pirates permeate Cape Cod's popular history, but so do unfamiliar artists, poets, entrepreneurs, inventors, and sea captains.

It Happened on Cape Cod introduces you to Captain Mayo, a Brewster sea captain who intended to smuggle Napoleon to America, and Jeremiah's Gutter—the Cape's first manmade canal. Other stories focus on "firsts," such as America's first transatlantic wireless telegraph message sent from Wellfleet, and the Cape's first lighthouse, commissioned by George Washington.

"The Graveyard of the Ocean" tells the tale of two ships sinking during the same violent storm, thus prompting the biggest Coast Guard rescue in history. When in Chatham, it's difficult not to reflect on this bittersweet tragedy once you realize that the stern of one of the ships rests just beyond the bar. "A Fair Island for Martha" will encourage you to remember the young child for whom the vineyard is named, and a pilgrimage to Wellfleet or Provincetown will be further enhanced after reading "The End of the *Whydah*" and "Ghost Ship Rising"—two stories that relay the account of the "Pirate Prince," "Black Sam" Bellamy, and the only sunken pirate treasure ever recovered by a dreamer who believed in it.

INTRODUCTION

Every town on the Cape has a fascinating history and a wealth of interesting stories, all worthy of inclusion in this book. Drawing on firsthand accounts, newspaper articles, and historical documents, *It Happened on Cape Cod* offers just a small sampling and cross-section of important military, maritime, scientific, and economic events that have impacted the development and history of the Cape in unique and interesting ways.

A FAIR ISLAND FOR YOUNG MARTHA

- 1602 -

WHEN COMPARED WITH THE FRENCH, SPANISH, AND Dutch, the English were very slow to take interest in colonizing North America. It was during the late 1500s that an enterprising group of Englishmen from Suffolk began to think about permanently settling in North America.

Captain Bartholomew Gosnold was instrumental in establishing the first permanent settlement in Jamestown, Virginia, but he is better known for exploring Cape Cod for the first time while leading the original prospecting expedition to Virginia in 1602. The story behind the discovery and naming of many significant landmarks around Cape Cod is told in the journal of Gabriel Archer, one of Gosnold's travel companions.

On Friday, March 26, 1602, Bartholomew Gosnold and his expedition set sail from Falmouth, England, for the New World. Aboard the *Concord* was a group of colonists, including eight mariners and twenty-three gentlemen adventurers, twelve of whom would later return to England with tales of their discoveries.

By early May the Labrador Current was pushing the rugged, 50-foot vessel southward along the coast of Maine and Massachusetts. The men took note of the diverse birds, for which they had no name in their English tongue. On Friday, May 14, the crew sighted their first land—a giant outcropping, which today is believed to have been the headland of Cape Ann.

After dropping anchor, Gosnold took out his spyglass to have a look around. It wasn't very long before he spotted a small boat carrying what he believed to be "distressed Christians" toward their ship. As the shallop drew closer, the crew was surprised to see it contained eight curious Indians, who were even more curiously dressed in European breeches and waistcoats.

They came in peace. Much to Gosnold's surprise, they were even able to speak many French, Spanish, and Portuguese words. Gabriel Archer noticed that the Indians understood their English much better than the Englishmen understood the Indians. It was unbeknownst to the Englishmen that the Indians had had sustained contact with "white men" for a very long time. The North American coast had been the site of summer camps for Portuguese, Basque, and Scandinavian fishermen for hundreds of years. Gosnold's men were by no means the first tourists to Cape Cod.

After friendly exchanges with the Indians, the crew decided to press on to their final destination in Virginia. Gosnold thanked the Indians for pointing them in the right direction, named the jetty of land Savage Rock, and "set sail westward, leaving them and their coast."

On May 14, 1602, the *Concord* sailed into the waters of Cape Cod and the crew once again sighted land. They initially believed the Cape to be an island because of the great gulf of water lying westward of it. Gosnold chose to name this large sound Shoal Hope for its shallow waters and hazardous sandy bottom.

It was somewhere along the Lower Cape, near present-day Truro or Wellfleet, that they dropped anchor, and a small group of men went ashore to see what the "island" had to offer. They found the land full of unripe strawberries, birch trees, and deep sand. Another friendly Indian lent them a helping hand in navigating the terrain, but the adventurers returned to the ship at nightfall with few stories.

Those who remained aboard the ship bragged that the fishing along the coast was at least as good as that found in Newfoundland. In fact, the men had caught so many fish that they had to throw a countless number back into the sea. Having taken a "great store of codfish," Gosnold decided to change the bay's name from Shoal Hope to Cape Cod—and the name stuck.

The next day the *Concord* sailed a little farther along the coast, then dropped anchor near a sandy beach so that a small expedition could once again go exploring. It was after hiking up the highest of hills that they realized this piece of land was not at all an island, but a mile-wide, sandy peninsula, separated from the mainland by the great Cape Cod Bay.

Having his bearings, the captain continued maneuvering the ship through hazardous shoals along the coast of the Cape and eventually landed on the coast near present-day Woods Hole in Falmouth. Standing on the buggy beach, Bartholomew Gosnold gazed out over the water and, like thousands of modern-day travelers do each summer, headed for the big island 7 miles off in the distance.

The large island seemed uninhabited; the Englishmen were unaware the Wampanoag Indians had been living there for thousands of years. The Wampanoags called the island *Noepe,* or "dry place amid waters." Gosnold's arrival marked the beginning of the Vineyard's European history and the beginning of the end of the Wampanoags—until more recent days.

The men went ashore on the morning of May 22, 1602. Finding this new island extremely pleasant, they decided to stay the night. Gabriel Archer wrote admiringly of the landscape and local nature. They found cranes and geese and took in an even better store of cod-fish than they had earlier in Cape Cod.

Its terrain was wooded and covered with wild grape vines, prompting Gosnold to name the beautiful island Martha's Vineyard, after his one-year-old daughter who had died a few years earlier. At Bury St. Edmonds in England, where young Martha is buried, the original gravestone marking her place of rest no longer exists; but her short life was immortalized in the name of one of the most popular holiday spots in America.

GOSNOLD'S HOPE

- 1602 -

In 1602, Elizabeth I was Queen of England. Her reign marked an age of adventure, during which the lands of North America were extensively explored and mapped by the French, Spanish, and English. Claiming and naming new land for one's monarch was the modus operandi for most European explorers. Englishman Bartholomew Gosnold went somewhat astray of protocol by naming the first island he discovered in the New World after his daughter, Martha, but he didn't forget about his queen.

It was May 24, 1602. Gosnold and his crew had spent the past three days exploring Martha's Vineyard. They liked the island and deemed it safe, but decided it was best to keep moving. They, after all, wanted to settle in Virginia.

After collecting a great store of codfish, the *Concord* doubled back around the west end of the Vineyard, sailing past the sweeping, clay cliffs of present-day Gay Head. The Englishmen, reminded of the chalky cliffs along the coastline of southern England, named this headland Dover Cliffs. By 1662, sailors had changed the name to "Gayhead," because of the gaily colored striations in the earth. Gayhead was subsequently split into two words, Gay Head, but has altogether reverted back to its Indian name, Aquinnah.

It took the entire night for the ship to pass through Vineyard Sound, and on the morning of May 25, Gosnold's expedition entered the waters of Buzzards Bay. Gabriel Archer found the scenery beautiful enough to write that it was "one of the stateliest sounds ever I was in."

The explorers found a chain of islands stretching from present-day Woods Hole to Rhode Island Sound, separating Vineyard Sound from Buzzards Bay. Gosnold and his expedition decided to create a permanent settlement on the most westerly of these islands and named it Elizabeth Island in honor of the queen. He believed it to be a great location for a trading post.

This small island, located only 14 miles from the coast of what is currently New Bedford, was surrounded by water, which afforded the group a certain amount of protection. The island was also minimally inhabited by the natives, who may have hunted or fished on these islands, but did not live there year-round. This extra safety measure added to the island's appeal. There was also a source of fresh water and a good supply of wood.

On May 28, Gosnold instructed several of his men to build a fort near a freshwater pond. The fort would act as a base of operations, while Gosnold and a few others went out exploring the island. During the next few days, the men at the base camp collected sassafras, sowed grain seeds, and made a flat-bottomed boat called a punt, for easy maneuvering over the marshy ponds.

Gosnold's expedition returned on May 31 with a canoe that had been left behind by fleeing Indians, but a few days later, they again set off to explore the mainland area near New Bedford. Upon his return to the fort, he showed off the gifts of furs, turtles, and hemp given to them by the courteous and attractive people on the "good-liest continent" he had ever seen.

Gosnold came up with an ambitious plan to leave twenty men behind to establish the trading post, while the others would return to England and bring back more provisions. The entire group spent the first four days of June working on the fort, but the buzz of activity piqued the Wampanoags' interest.

On June 5, while most of the men were aboard the ship, a group of fifty natives equipped with bows and arrows came ashore. There were only eight men in the camp at the time, including Gabriel Archer, who thought to approach the Indians with his musket and gesture to them with an option of peace or war. The Indians had come in peace, and the groups sat down together.

Captain Gosnold made his way from the boat to the island with twelve others. He was greeted as the leader of the English group and then gave the Indian chief a straw hat, which he immediately put on, and a pair of knives, which he marveled at. It was this courtesy that Archer claims "made them all in love with us."

After a rainy day spent sitting around on the ship, the men were finally able to get back to work on June 7. The Indian chief and his troops came around once again and were invited to stay for dinner, during which the Englishmen had a good laugh at the natives' reaction to the strong mustard nipping at their noses. The environment was relaxed and relations seemed good with the locals.

The eighth of June was the day of reckoning. Supplies were to be divided up between the ship and the fort—and it didn't take long for a controversy to arise. Those staying with the trading post claimed that only six weeks of supplies had been issued for what might be up to a six-month wait for fresh provisions. There was also talk of the captain pilfering the goods for himself while in England and the ship not returning at all.

On June 10, nine resolute men stayed on Elizabeth Island to finish building the storehouse, while Captain Gosnold took the *Concord* and sailed away from the fort, with the intention of bringing back firewood to the camp. He left the men with only three meals and a promise to return the next day. While he was gone, the Indians paid another visit to the island out of uneasy curiosity. This, coupled with a sneaking suspicion that they might have been stranded, left the settlers feeling even more uncertain about staying behind.

A full day passed and there was no sign of the ship. Having eaten their rations of food, the men had to find a way to sustain themselves. Against their better judgment, they split up to find food. Late in the evening, one group was assaulted by Indians and spent the stormy night hiding out, lost in the thick brush. On the morning of June 12, the groups were joyously reunited, but there was still no sign of Captain Gosnold.

Terror struck at their hearts. Men who were, just the day before, extremely confident about making this the first permanent English settlement in the New World now spoke of revolt. Late in the day on June 12, when hope was fading away with the sun, Gabriel Archer and the group of eight planters finally heard the captain summon to them. They were never happier. In the end, it was determined that the group simply did not have enough provisions to sustain both the ship and the colony. On June 18, 1602, all thirty-two explorers boarded the *Concord* and headed back to England, arriving in Exmouth on July 23.

Elizabeth Island remained an English territory and became a landmark for future explorers, but all that exists of Gosnold's settlement is a 60-foot monument made of native boulders, marking the spot of the original fortress. Elizabeth Island is presently known by its Indian name, Cuttyhunk, but the term Elizabeth has spread to include the entire chain of islands, which were included in the land grant given by King James I to the Council for New England in 1606.

It is believed that Elizabeth Island served as the setting for William Shakespeare's play, *The Tempest*. Many believe the bard had access to Gosnold's travel journals or maps, and just might have immortalized this small, obscure New World island in a fine piece of Renaissance literature. While the colony didn't quite turn out the way Gosnold had hoped, Cuttyhunk remains settled to this day, and its primary town is named Gosnold, commemorating its English founder.

THE KETTLE CONTROVERSY

- 1605 -

SAMUEL DE CHAMPLAIN WAS A seventeenth-century French explorer and skillful navigator who mapped and claimed much of northeastern North America for King Henry IV of France. As "geographer royal," Champlain developed a pattern of exploring and mapping a region for several months, then returning to France to relay his discoveries to the king and gather more funding. He crossed the Atlantic at least twenty times in his lifetime and had an intense desire to "obtain knowledge of different countries, regions and realms."

In 1603, Champlain was sent to New France (present-day Canada and Maine), to further Jacques Cartier's discoveries from a half-century earlier. He first sailed around Cape Cod and Martha's Vineyard in 1604 and then returned again in 1605 and 1606.

It was during the later two visits that Champlain surveyed the coastline and drew up what many consider to be the oldest recognizable map of what is now New England. His map refers to Cape Cod as Cap Blanc, or "the white cape," so named because of its light-colored sand. Apparently, he was unaware (or perhaps just ignoring the fact) that Bartholomew Gosnold had beaten him to the punch a few years earlier and had named the bay Cape Cod.

Champlain was by no means the first European to have made contact with the Indians, but few earlier written accounts are in existence. One of the earliest mentions of Cape Cod is by the Italian explorer Giovanni da Verrazzano, who discovered many places along the Atlantic coast during his 1524 expedition. Verrazzano mapped his voyages and named many of these places in letters to King Francis I of France. It's also likely the English-funded explorer, John Cabot, encountered Cape Cod on his way to somewhere else.

It was, however, Samuel de Champlain who spent three and a half years charting the coastline and observing the inhabitants between Nova Scotia and Cape Cod. He noted in his journal that all previous descriptions of Cape Cod offered very little in comparison to his own. It is not surprising then, that Champlain provided the first written account of high crime on Cape Cod.

Champlain was an incessant journal-keeper and published a story of his travels between the years of 1604 and 1612 in a book titled *The Voyages of Sieur de Champlain.* By his own account, he felt that he did his duty as best he could to document all that he saw, in greater detail than anyone had before him. His tale of a violent skirmish over a kettle is the first written documentation of theft and murder on Cape Cod.

It was the spring of 1605. Pierre du Gua, the French governor of Acadia, rallied a group of colonists to leave St. Croix Island, near Maine, and go in search of a new place to settle. Champlain went along as the ship cartographer. As the expedition sailed south from New France, he mapped the coast from Maine to Massachusetts.

Along the way, the colonists made friends with some of the local Indians, visited their villages, and even allowed some of the

Wampanoags to join the crew. Champlain began to lose his trust and admiration for the locals after several conflicts, one of which resulted in the death of a crewmember.

The ship dropped anchor in present-day Nauset Harbor in Orleans, and a few of the crew went ashore in search of fresh water. After just a few minutes, they came running back to the ship, screaming in French for their mates to open fire on the Indians who were chasing them.

Sure enough, there were several Wampanoags in close pursuit, with bows and arrows in hand. Despite the language barrier, the Wampanoags on the ship could tell there was trouble. All but one, who was detained, leaped overboard into the water, fearing for their safety.

By the time the sailors aboard the ship loaded their muskets, a Wampanoag had shot one of the fleeing men in the back with an arrow, killing him. Seeing this, the musketeers began firing at the Indians from the ship, scaring them off into the woods. Their efforts were too little, too late. All they could do was retrieve their dead crewmember and try to figure out what had gone wrong.

Champlain wrote in his journal that one of the Indians had stolen the kettle in which the sailors had planned to carry fresh water back to the ship. A chase ensued, but the Indians were too swift for the Frenchmen. It is unclear how the pursuit turned against the sailors, but there is no doubt the theft escalated into an all-out skirmish, resulting in the first murder on Cape Cod.

Later that day a group of Wampanoags came to the boat with their leader to reconcile the matter, blaming the theft on another tribe. The Frenchmen released the Indian they had been holding captive and made their peace, but from that point on, Champlain claimed the Wampanoags were not to be trusted. "They are great thieves," he wrote, "and, if they cannot lay hold of any thing with their hands, they try to do so with their feet. . . . It is necessary to be on one's guard against this people, and live in a state of distrust with them, yet without letting them perceive it."

There is no written account of this situation from the Indian perspective. Maybe the natives were already feeling encroached upon or had prior bad experiences with the "white man." Maybe the sailors provoked the "tawny men." There is also the possibility that an Indian did steal the kettle. No one knows for certain the truth of the matter, except perhaps the dead man.

This story is just one example of how cultural misunderstandings, language barriers, and, quite often, the Europeans' ill-considered actions ignited confrontations with the local Indians. It is hard to say with any certainty the accuracy of Champlain's words or to pinpoint who really instigated the trouble, but it is safe to assume the Indians had experienced both gracious and hostile white men by the time Champlain arrived.

These stories of conflict were often used by the early colonials to define the natives as "savages," and, whether exaggerated or not, they have carried over into popular history. Fifteen years after Champlain's brush with the local Indians, the pilgrims had their own theft-related "first encounter" with the Wampanoags—only this time the Indians weren't the culprits.

LAW AND ORDER:
THE MAYFLOWER COMPACT

- 1620 -

THE MAYFLOWER COMPACT IS BELIEVED TO BE ONE of the earliest examples of democracy in America. It was written on November 11, 1620, by William Bradford, one of the pilgrims aboard the *Mayflower,* a ship bound for Virginia to establish a private permanent colony. These early settlers brought with them strong religious beliefs and social traditions that set the tone for America's first legitimate government.

It was during the reign of King James I (1603–1625) that a Puritanical religious group wanted to separate itself from the Church of England. Religious upheaval and persecution caused these "Separatists" to leave the Nottinghamshire area of England for the more religiously tolerant country of the Netherlands. There, they hoped to find religious freedom to live their lives in accordance with their strict beliefs.

The Pilgrims worshipped briefly in Amsterdam, then moved to a congregation in Leiden, where they remained for ten years. A very poor quality of life, combined with looming religious persecution and the potential loss of their children's English identity, were the primary reasons for relocating to the British colony of Virginia.

While in Holland, the Pilgrims purchased a ship called the *Speedwell*, in which they returned to England in May of 1620. They then made contact with the owner of a sizeable cargo ship called the *Mayflower*, which was chartered by several merchants seeking financial gain in the New World. The groups were given permission to settle in Northern Virginia—currently the New York Hudson River area. In August 1620, the two ships met in Southampton, England, and set sail for America.

During the first attempt to make the crossing, the *Speedwell* leaked so badly that the expedition was forced to return to England. The Separatists cut their losses and sold the *Speedwell*, and 102 passengers crowded onto the *Mayflower* to brave the Atlantic in one ship. The group included English merchants, skilled craftsmen, hired colonists, and people from the Leiden congregation. Those in search of religious freedom were nicknamed "Saints" while those seeking business opportunities were referred to as "Strangers." It wasn't until the 1800s that these early settlers were collectively referred to as Pilgrims.

The Saints and Strangers boarded the *Mayflower* on September 6, 1620, and departed from Plymouth, England, for the second attempt to journey to the new land. According to the only two existing accounts of the voyage, they spent two months crossing the treacherous seas in a crowded, disease-infested ship. Words of mutiny were not uncommon.

When land was finally sighted on November 9, the crew of the *Mayflower* realized they were in Cape Cod, well north of Virginia. After a few attempts to press on, they determined the weather was too rough to risk heading south. On the cold morning of November 11, 1620, the *Mayflower* dropped anchor in a protected harbor on the tip of Cape Cod, near the Indian site of Paomet, now known as Provincetown.

Some of the Pilgrims were unhappy with the decision to stay in Cape Cod, because they did not have England's permission to settle the area. A few Strangers decided they were no longer bound by contract to the stockholders. Rebellion was brewing. Mindful of the failed settlement in Jamestown, Virginia, just a few years earlier, the Pilgrims agreed they would not make the same mistake. The group understood the need for a centralized government and strong leadership, so they created a document that would establish a temporary government until they could get permission from England to colonize the area.

This short contract, called the Mayflower Compact, had long-term results and reads as follows:

> *Agreement Between the Settlers at New Plymouth:*
> *1620*
> IN THE NAME OF GOD, AMEN. *We, whose names are underwritten, the Loyal Subjects of our dread Sovereign Lord King James, by the Grace of God, of Great Britain, France, and Ireland, King, Defender of the Faith, &c. Having undertaken for the Glory of God, and Advancement of the Christian Faith, and the Honour of our King and Country, a voyage to plant the first Colony in the northern Parts of Virginia; Do by these Presents, solemnly and mutually, in the Presence of God and one another, covenant and combine*

ourselves together into a civil Body Politick, for our better Ordering and Preservation, and Furtherance of the Ends aforesaid: And by Virtue hereof do enact, constitute, and frame, such just and equal Laws, Ordinances, Acts, Constitutions, and Officers, from time to time, as shall be thought most meet and convenient for the general Good of the Colony; unto which we promise all due Submission and Obedience.

IN WITNESS whereof we have hereunto subscribed our names at Cape-Cod the eleventh of November, in the Reign of our Sovereign Lord King James, of England, France, and Ireland, the eighteenth, and of Scotland the fifty-fourth, Anno Domini; 1620.

While most historians agree the Mayflower Compact was not a constitution in the sense of being a fundamental framework of government, its importance lies in the Pilgrims' firm belief that government was a covenant between men. In order for a government to be legitimate, it had to be recognized and consented to by those it intended to govern. The Pilgrims chose to govern themselves according to the will of the majority.

On November 11, 1620, forty-one men boarded the *Mayflower* and signed an agreement that created a "government of the people, by the people, and for the people," and established the basis for America's first written laws.

EARLY EXPLORATIONS:
PILGRIM'S SPRING AND CORN HILL

- 1620 -

THE PILGRIMS FIRST DROPPED ANCHOR ON THE SANDY, desolate tip of Cape Cod near present-day Provincetown—not in Plymouth as popular history holds. Firsthand accounts of the earliest explorations of these settlers are offered in writing by two of the men who made the crossing, William Bradford and Edward Winslow. The presence of these English pioneers is felt and seen in historic monuments all over the northern neck of Cape Cod. The plaques at Pilgrim's Spring and Corn Hill in Truro commemorate two of the first places they made their mark.

After signing the Mayflower Compact on Saturday, November 11, 1620, the Pilgrims began exploring the area they were planning to call home. They were well aware that they had landed in Cape Cod and that their charter did not permit settlement of the region north of what is now New York City. But since the icy winter would soon be settling in, they decided not to travel any farther south and sought an official charter to create a colony in New England.

Sixteen men went ashore in a shallop, or small boat, to seek out a place where they could settle and build their new colony. The group was greeted by rolling hills and moors that must have been vaguely reminiscent of their homeland. Taking a quick look around, the men found sandy dunes, juniper trees, and wild grass that ran all the way down to the water in some places—and not much else. With firewood in hand, the party returned to the ship at nightfall and reported having seen no person and no sign of habitation, only marshy ponds and thousands of birds.

The next day, everyone remained on the *Mayflower* in honor of the Sabbath, during which they offered up prayers of thanksgiving for their safe arrival. The following two days were spent bringing the women and children ashore. The carpenters set to work repairing a badly damaged sailboat, while the women, under adequate guard, did laundry, and the kids ran off two months' worth of pent-up energy.

Significant expeditions, or "discoveries," of the coastline around present-day Truro began on Wednesday, November 15, 1620, and are described in full in the document titled *Mourt's Relations*. Captain Myles Standish, William Bradford, Stephen Hopkins, and Edward Tilley, along with twelve others, began exploring the narrow, northern neck of Cape Cod on foot.

It was this same day the search party first sighted the locals, but the six natives and their dog disappeared into the forest as the group approached. After pursuing the Indians in vain, the men camped on the beach for the night.

Unable to locate the Indians the following day, the party became more interested in finding fresh drinking water. After wandering through hills of thick underbrush, they came upon a fresh-water spring in a clearing at the bottom of a hill. The words on a modern-day plaque at Pilgrim's Spring are taken from firsthand accounts: "about ten o'clock we came into a deepe valley brush, wood-gaille and long grass, through which we found little paths or tracks and there we saw a deere and found springs of fresh water of which we were heartily glad and sat us downe and drunke our first New England water." Edward Winslow, a member of the expedition, wrote that they drank "with as much delight as ever we drunk drink in all our lives."

Rejuvenated, the men pressed on through the small hills, and later that day they came upon mounds of sand that they thought to be Indian graves. The heaps seemed so newly formed that they decided to dig down to see what was below. They found two baskets of corn, "some yellow, and some red and others mixed with blue." This discovery, along with the nearby cornfields, inspired them to name the area Corn Hill.

The fields and the buried baskets of corn had not been abandoned, as the Pilgrims wanted to believe, but had only been stored underground to be used the following season by the local Pamet Indians. Knowing they had no way of getting seed for the next year, the Pilgrims justified stealing the corn by saying they were only "borrowing" it and would repay the owner, as soon as they found out who it was. Today, a small bronze marker notes the historic spot where the Pilgrims took as much corn as they could carry back to the *Mayflower*.

After returning to the ship and reporting what they had found, the weather turned frigid and stormy. Despite several inches of snow and freezing winds, the Pilgrims continued looting the stockpiled mounds around Corn Hill during the course of the next two weeks. When all was said and done, they had "borrowed" ten bushels of corn.

The Pilgrims considered this cache of corn a blessing, and it did help to sustain them through the following year in Plymouth. It was, however, these presumptuous acts of pilfering that made for an interesting first encounter with the Indians on December 8, 1620, further south in Eastham.

THE FIRST ENCOUNTER

- 1620 -

FOR ALMOST A MONTH, the Pilgrims had been searching the Cape in vain for a suitable place to build their new colony. On Wednesday, December 6, 1620, seventeen "discoverers" took the shallop out for a third and final expedition. This group included Captain Myles Standish, John Carver, William Bradford, Edward Winslow, Edward Doten, John Tilley, Edward Tilley, John Howland, Richard Warren, Stephen Hopkins, John Allerton, and Thomas English. Five of the sailors from the *Mayflower* crew, including master gunner Robert Coppin, were also part of this expedition.

The men set sail southward along the West Coast, intending to "circulate that deep bay of Cape Cod." The weather was so cold that the spraying seawater froze to their clothes, making them feel, as one man recorded, "as if they had been glazed." Assaulted by the brutal December elements, the men made very slow headway against the frigid wind. They continued looking for rivers and bays that might be deep enough to dock the *Mayflower* near high ground and fresh water.

The Pilgrims sailed beyond what is present-day Wellfleet, and by nightfall they were approaching the area that is now Eastham. Edward Doten noted ten or twelve Indians busy doing something on the beach, but when the natives saw the explorers coming, they ran off into the woods.

The discoverers brought their battered little boat to shore. It was getting dark and they decided to set up camp and spend the night on the beach. They built a much-needed fire and went about constructing a barricade, using logs and thick pine boughs. The barricade, which was as tall as a man and open on one side, protected them from a possible attack and sheltered them from the wind and the cold.

The fire was built in the middle. The men could tell from the smoke of the Indians' campfire that they were about 5 miles away. It was safe to assume that if the Pilgrims could see the Indians' fire, then the Indians could certainly see theirs. Guards were put in place and the men tried to get some sleep.

The next day was spent exploring the area in two groups; one went by water and the other by land. The first group took the shallop and sailed along the coast, in hopes of finding a substantial river. The second group trekked through the hills, following Indian tracks past a graveyard, abandoned Indian summer houses, and cornfields. They eventually came upon the place where the Indians had been the night before and learned that they had been cleaning a large black fish like a grampus, or dolphin. Overall, they considered the area uninhabitable.

Once again, the Pilgrims' search for a new dwelling site proved futile. There were no rivers and no suitable land. Cape Cod really was just a marshy bay.

As the sun was setting, the two groups met back at the shallop. They had their supper and made their barricade as they had done the night before. Around midnight they heard a "hideous and great cry," after which the guardsman called "Arm! Arm!" The men jerked from their sleep and grabbed their muskets. After shooting off a few rounds into the air, the noise stopped. One of the seamen convinced the others that he heard these same screeching noises from wolves, or similar wild beasts, while in Newfoundland. The group attempted to go back to sleep, but it must have been a restless remainder of the night.

In the wee hours of the morning on Friday, December 8, 1620, the Pilgrims said their prayers, had breakfast, and began carrying their things down to the boat to move on. All of a sudden, they heard the same "great and strange cry" that had woken them only five hours earlier. One of the men in the company came running, shouting "Men, Indians! Indians!"

Unfortunately, several of the Pilgrims had already packed their guns into the boat, and as they scurried off to recover their arms from the shallop, the Indians sent arrows sailing into the camp and began to descend upon the barricade. At this point, only four men in the camp had loaded guns. It was five o'clock in the morning and the sun had not come up yet, so two of the men shot into the darkness, while the others stood ready to fire as soon as they had a visible shot. Once the other pilgrims retrieved their guns from the boat, they began to fire into the woods, scaring the Indians off as quickly as they had come. Surprisingly, no one was killed or injured on either side despite this quick and violent exchange of fire.

Arrows had pierced the barricade and made holes in all of the men's clothing hanging on its walls, but since not one of the men was hurt in this conflict, the Pilgrims believed they were protected by God's divine providence. They sent a bundle of the Indian arrows back to England, telling of their vanquished enemies.

A plaque located at Eastham's Town Hall commemorates this skirmish between the Pilgrims and Indians. As already mentioned, this was by no means the first meeting between Europeans and the natives of Cape Cod, but the Pilgrims' first interaction with the locals left such an impression that they decided to name the location First Encounter Beach, which it remains to this day.

APTUCXET TRADING POST: AMERICA'S FIRST FREE ENTERPRISE

- 1627 -

THE PILGRIMS HAD A HAND IN SHAPING many different aspects of American history. It is well known that they created the Mayflower Compact, thus setting the tone for the democratic foundation of the country. But lesser known is their establishment of the Aptucxet Trading Post, the first recorded commercial trading site in America, which many consider to be the economic cornerstone of the United States.

The Pilgrims had been in the New World for only two years. It was the winter of 1622 and they were in dire need of supplementary food. They had not yet mastered the New England climate and soil, and as a result, their crops weren't producing enough to get them through the winter. A group went out in search of food, and after trekking 20 miles to the south of Plymouth, they came upon a Wampanoag village on the bank of the Manomet River, just at the edge of the Cape.

There, they bought so much corn they were unable to carry it all back to Plymouth. They stored what they couldn't carry with a native named Cawnacome, with intentions of returning for it. The men deposited the first supply of corn back at the plantation and returned to get the rest, but upon their arrival, they learned that Cawnacome was fishing 3 miles farther down river at Aptucxet, a name which means, "little trap in the river." This was how the Pilgrims learned of the area in which they were to pursue their first business venture a few years later.

It is important to know that before coming to the New World in 1620, the Pilgrims had made an agreement with the English company that had funded both their passage to America and the settlement of the new colony. The contract with the London Company originally stated that the settlers would own their own homes, own stock, and would work for the company five days a week; two days a week, they could work for themselves. This seemed an acceptable arrangement to the Pilgrims.

Plans were in place for the "Saints" and "Strangers" to set sail on the *Mayflower,* but shortly before leaving for America, the terms of the contract were changed—to the extreme benefit of the London Company. The new agreement stated that no one owned anything in the new colony until all debt was repaid. The Pilgrims, having little choice but to go, signed themselves into seven years of servitude to the London Company.

In the first few years, the London Company continued to subsidize more settlers from whom they required repayment, therefore adding to the debt of the original colonists. If that wasn't bad enough, they increased interest rates on what was owed. The debt was growing as fast as the colonists could pay it off, so they had to come up with some way to make money.

A few of the Pilgrims recalled the winter they had gone in search of Cawnacome and ended up at Aptucxet. During that journey, they had learned that the Manomet and Scusset Rivers provided easy access between Cape Cod Bay in the East and Buzzards Bay in the West. They now had a shortcut across the shoulder of the Cape, rather than having to sail the whole way around it.

This safe inland location, and the shorter, safer route to the regions south of the Cape, gave the group an idea to erect a small trading post. Aptucxet's fresh water source further encouraged them to choose this site, as it enabled them to leave someone there year-round to guard the goods. They received permission from England to set up shop.

A wood-framed building of hewn oak planks was built using a construction style typical of the seventeenth century. It was anchored into the ground with posts, and a wooden latticework (called wattle) was filled in with a mixture of mud, clay, animal dung, and straw (called daub) to create the walls. This one-room shop might have been whitewashed to protect it from the elements, but it might also have been sided with clapboard, like the homes of Plymouth Plantation. One thing is for certain about the trading post: Its roof was made of wood boards and was not thatched, as were many of the early plantation homes. At the time Aptucxet was built, straw roofs were recognized as a serious fire hazard and were illegal in the colony.

The Pilgrims started shipping furs to England by the boatload. They also began trading up and down every river, bay, and inlet south to the Connecticut River. They traded with the Dutch in New Amsterdam (present-day New York) and with the Indians. The booming trade business soon required the development of a currency system, so Aptucxet began using the wampum (a cylindrical, polished fragment of a clam's shell), making it the first commercial enterprise in the New World to use local currency on a regular basis. The Pilgrims may have conceived, set up, and run the business, but the profits turned at Aptucxet belonged to the London Company. It was a way of paying off the Pilgrims' debt.

This small business venture set the stage for the important events that were to occur the following year. It was, according to Governor William Bradford of Plymouth, the Aptucxet Trading Post that saved the colony financially. Prior to 1627, very little North American trade was conducted by the private business sector. French and Spanish settlements were funded by their kings, so all revenue went directly to the crown. On the other hand, Dutch and English colonies were financed by private investment companies whose investors reaped the profits. Such was the case at Plymouth, but things were about to change.

In 1627, the Pilgrims' contract with the London Company expired, and eight residents of Plymouth drew up a contract of their own terms. William Bradford, William Brewster, Myles Standish, Edward Winslow, John Howland, Thomas Prence, John Alden, and Isaac Allerton proposed that they (along with four others from London) would pay off all debts for everyone in the colony, which was around 250 people, if they could have ownership of Aptucxet, two boats, and everything in stock. They also wanted exclusive rights to trade in the area. In other words, they wanted a monopoly.

The London Company wanted their money back, so they had no choice but to agree to the new terms and signed the contract in the fall of 1627. The Pilgrims' negotiation of their own contract made the Aptucxet Trading Post America's first private business contract, and the country's first private, small business.

The site of the original Aptucxet Trading Post is located just over the canal on the Cape side, in present-day Bourne. The original building was destroyed in a hurricane in 1635 and supposedly rebuilt. The fresh-water spring is still visible today. Though few detailed records exist of the importance of this little trading post, there is no denying the part it played in the development of free enterprise in America.

THE PILGRIMS RETURN

- 1646 -

EASTHAM, ONE OF THE CAPE'S FOUR ORIGINAL TOWNS, may not be its oldest, but it is the only one founded entirely by settlers of Plymouth Colony. In 1620, when the Pilgrims first landed in the New World, Myles Standish and his expedition had a conflict with the local Nauset Indians at present-day Eastham. The group was so affected by this experience that they named the site First Encounter Beach and abandoned the area. It would be more than twenty years before the Pilgrims would make their way back to Cape Cod from the mainland.

By the 1630s, Plymouth Colony was established and the Pilgrims' debts to the London Company were paid off, but many had become dissatisfied with their lifestyles. The soil was poor, the land grants were small, and Plymouth was getting extremely crowded. At one time or another, many of the original settlers contemplated returning to the Cape, but two decades passed before the wheels were set in motion.

In 1640, Governor William Bradford defined the Cape in a patent to the Earl of Warwick in England. He described "that tract of land lying between sea and sea," using its Indian name of Nawsett, which means "at the river's bend." It included most of the present-day Lower Cape: Brewster, Harwich, Eastham, Wellfleet, Provincetown, Truro, Orleans, and parts of Chatham. The lands of Nawsett were reserved, by government decree, for "Purchasers" and "Old Comers"—those who paid the colonists' way out of debt, and those who came to the New World aboard the first three ships: *Mayflower, Fortune,* and *Anne.*

In 1643, an expedition was sent to Nawsett to determine the potential of moving the entire Plymouth colony back to the place where they had first stepped foot in the New World. After a few excursions through the region, and despite finding many harbors and an abundance of shellfish, it was decided that the area could not sustain such a large number of people. Instead, the colony purchased tracts of land from local Indians, and in April of 1644, the colonial court of Plymouth gave permission for seven families from Plymouth (forty-nine people in all) to "go to dwell at Nauset."

The group included both Old Comers and Purchasers. Edward Bangs, Eastham's first treasurer, was both. He was born in England and had arrived in Plymouth Colony in 1623, aboard the *Anne.* He became a great landowner and was licensed to sell wine and strong waters in Nauset, "provided it bee for the refreshment of the English and not the Indians." He died in Eastham at eighty-seven years of age.

Josias Cook, the town's first constable, and Richard Higgins, a highway surveyor, were from two of the seven original families to settle in Nauset, and both died in Eastham, well into old age. It was, however, Deacon John Doane who outlived them all. He was 110 years old when he died in 1707, and tradition holds that he was rocked in a cradle during several of his final years.

Nicholas Snow, a true "gentleman of Eastham" and the town's first clerk, came to the New World aboard the *Anne* and was married to Constance Hopkins, who came on the *Mayflower*. Her fellow passengers, Giles Hopkins (no relation) and Lieutenant Joseph Rogers were also among the earliest families to settle in Eastham and are both buried alongside Constance in Eastham Cove Burying Ground.

It was under the leadership of Thomas Prence that the town grew and prospered. Eastham's earliest economy was based on agriculture and fishing. The fertile, sandy soil was perfect for growing asparagus and turnips; so much so that Eastham was considered the asparagus capital of the world well into the twentieth century.

Thomas Prence was born in England and arrived at Plymouth Plantation aboard the *Fortune* in 1621, shortly after the first Thanksgiving was held. He made his early fortune as one of the eight members of the trade monopoly of Aptucxet, but was better known for his leadership roles within Plymouth Colony. Following the death of William Bradford in 1657, Prence was elected governor of Plymouth. He chose, however, to live away from the colony.

Prence and his wife, Patience Brewster (daughter of Elder William Brewster), were residing in Duxbury when it was decided that seven families, including his own, would establish a new town out on the Cape. His farm, which included the present-day town of Eastham, was said to have been the "richest land in the place." His property holdings were extensive; Prence owned land around modern-day Harwich, Brewster, Wellfleet, and Truro. He planted a pear tree, brought with him from England, near his farmhouse, where it stood until it was blown over in 1849.

Prence was considered a just and qualified leader of the town, but his Puritanical beliefs triggered intolerance and open criticism of most other religions. When the Quaker missionaries arrived on Cape

Cod from England in the 1650s, they received the same sort of rejection that had driven the Puritans from their motherland to the New World. Prence enforced the imprisonment and punishment of anyone who supported the Quakers. In an ironic twist of fate, his daughter eventually married a Quaker and provided him with several Quaker grandchildren.

Once settled by this group of young and able businessmen, it took less than two years for Nauset to be designated an official township. It was incorporated on June 2, 1646, and was officially named Eastham in 1651. But as early as 1654, the large township was starting to be divided. A few Old Comers had claims to the western half of Eastham, which soon became Harwich, while William Nickerson claimed what would eventually become Chatham.

By the late 1700s, towns like Wellfleet and Orleans were also breaking off from Eastham, making what was originally the Cape's largest town one of its smallest—but never mind the size. It is to Eastham that many of the Pilgrims returned and lived out the rest of their lives. The surnames of America's earliest settlers continue to permeate the town's census list and its cemeteries. Here, and throughout other Cape Cod burial grounds, you will find some of the country's earliest sculptural carvings and inscriptions on some of its oldest tombstones.

THE END OF THE *WHYDAH*

- 1717 -

"BLACK SAM" BELLAMY WASN'T ALWAYS A PIRATE. He was born in 1690 and grew up dirt poor on the docks of Plymouth, England, a breeding ground for pirates. There is no doubt he heard stories of remarkable wealth and saw, firsthand, the great seafaring bandits such as the grandfather of piracy, Henry Avery, and the crown-sponsored bandits, John Hawkins and Francis Drake, coming and going from the Plymouth port.

Unhappy with his life in the bottom tiers of English society, Bellamy made his way to the New World for a new beginning. He arrived in Cape Cod in 1714, at the age of twenty-four. It wasn't long before he met and fell in love with a local girl, Maria Hallett, and began spending a lot of time at the Great Island Tavern—a smuggler's den full of black-market goods, located on a small island 2 miles from Wellfleet. It was here that Bellamy first heard tales of sunken Spanish treasure off the coast of Florida.

It didn't take much to convince a jeweler named Paulsgrave Williams to finance Bellamy's venture. They bought a sloop and gathered a crew, but unfortunately, by the time the *Marianne* reached Florida, the gold had been recovered by a variety of buccaneers. Spaniards, English privateers, and pirates of the Caribbean had left nothing for Bellamy and Williams.

Disappointed, but not discouraged, Bellamy rallied his men to become official "looters of nations, free men, Pirates!" They hoisted the Jolly Roger, a black flag emblazoned with a skull and crossbones, and Black Sam Bellamy was on his way to becoming one of America's most feared and revered pirates.

Bellamy learned the art of high-sea crime from pirate-turned-pirate-hunter Benjamin Hornigold while spending time carousing with another student, the infamous Edward "Blackbeard" Teach. By early 1717, Bellamy had become the terror of the Caribbean. He seized booty from more than fifty ships and had more than 200 men under his command. He also possessed five ships, including the *Whydah,* which he personally captained.

Bellamy had spent several days chasing the *Whydah* around the Caribbean, before finally capturing the ship of every pirate's dream: a galley with a huge cargo space full of gold and silver, and loaded with armament. Black Sam and his crew decided it was time to retire. The plan was to sail north to Maine after retrieving Maria from Wellfleet, then live off their spoils. No one expected the tragedy that lay ahead.

As the pack of pirates made their way from the Caribbean to Cape Cod, they plundered every ship they encountered. By the early morning of April 26, 1717, the *Whydah* was bursting at the seams with booty: elephant tusks, molasses, and rum, not to mention precious coins and gold bars. "Could it get any better?" Black Sam thought to himself. Of course it could!

As they approached Nantucket, the crew seized a merchant ship from Dublin, which was carrying 7,000 gallons of Madeira wine.

Much to the dismay of the *Mary Anne*'s captain, Bellamy's men boarded the ship and forced it to join the *Whydah* on a northwesterly course—but only after indulging in the captain's private stash of wine! The wine was a fine seizure, but Bellamy was thinking more of Maria when he steered the ships toward Wellfleet, a fatal move that marked the beginning of the end of the *Whydah.*

As the heavily laden ship approached what is present-day Chatham, fog was setting in. Knowing the waters were shallow and the shoals dangerous in this part of the Cape, Bellamy bided his time and waited for a break in the weather. When a small sloop named the *Fisher* slowed down near the *Whydah,* its captain had the misfortune of admitting to knowing the waters. It was already late in the afternoon, so Bellamy sent a few men aboard to seize the *Fisher* to help navigate the *Whydah* and *Mary Anne* through the potentially treacherous waters.

Slowly they made their way up the east coast of the Cape, with *Mary Anne* leading the way. The wine-filled, hundred-ton galley was followed by the *Whydah,* and the *Fisher* brought up the rear. As it grew darker, the fog grew thicker and the waves began rising. The *Mary Anne* fell behind. It was late April and Black Sam assumed storm season was over so he forced the ships to press on, not realizing a powerful arctic wind blowing down from Canada was about to hit them head on.

By nightfall, the *Whydah* was out of sight of the *Mary Anne* and the *Fisher,* both of which had run aground. Their crews were arrested the next morning and jailed in Eastham. The *Whydah* had to keep going north, since this particular type of ship, a galley, could not handle high winds. Due north, however, was impossible. The seventy-mile-per-hour winds propelled the ship west toward land, into the breakers.

Over and over, the words "Breakers! Breakers!" were screamed above the howling rain. Bellamy ordered the men to turn the boat around and drop the main anchor, hoping they could ride out the storm without hitting land. The pirates made several valiant attempts to turn the ship into the waves to avoid being capsized. It worked a few times, but inevitably, the strength of Mother Nature was just too much for the 146 mortals aboard the *Whydah*. The ship ran aground only 500 feet from shore.

A little before midnight on April 26, 1717, the ship rolled and the fate of all aboard, including Black Sam Bellamy, was sealed.

Waves began heaving over the boat, dumping tons of water onto the deck and sweeping many of the pirates out to sea. The main mast broke off and floated away. Water quickly filled the holds and cargo area below. Anyone lucky enough to escape drowning below deck would not have lasted more than a few minutes in the frigid water and then would have had to struggle 500 feet to shore and up the steep hillside.

As the *Whydah* flipped over, all the valuables in the cargo space crashed about the ship. Many of the crewmen were crushed. Even worse, some were pinned to the bottom of the ocean by cannons and other heavy, quick-sinking objects. Their spoils became their head-stones. In the blink of an eye, 144 lives were lost.

The next morning more than a hundred bodies washed ashore—mutilated, swollen, unrecognizable. It is said that only two men survived. Did Black Sam go down with his ship or was he one of the survivors? No one knows for sure. As for the pirates sent from the *Whydah* to seize the *Mary Anne* and the *Fisher,* their fate was no better than those aboard the doomed ship. On October 22, 1717, the group was tried in the Boston Courthouse and eventually hung for their participation in piracy.

The treasure of the *Whydah* remained a legend for more than 250 years. It took Barry Clifford, a boyhood dreamer and a pirate in his own right, to continue the *Whydah*'s story, which is relayed later in "Ghost Ship Rising."

KEEPING THE BRITISH AT BAY

- 1779 -

FALMOUTH, NAMED FOR BARTHOLOMEW GOSNOLD'S HOMETOWN of Falmouth, England, was incorporated in 1686 and was one of the few Cape towns fired upon by the British during the Revolutionary War. Falmouth Harbor served as the stage for British raids during the years leading up to and throughout the war.

Cape Cod was drawn into the colonies' plight for freedom when Britain banned the use of Boston's port after locals had seized a British ship and dumped its contents into the harbor. After the infamous Tea Party, residents of Cape Cod contributed to the provisions needed to sustain Boston during this blockade.

The American Revolution began the following year, in 1775, when British troops were sent to destroy the shops in Concord, Massachusetts. Along the way, 700 militiamen warded off more than 1,700 of England's finest—and the war had begun. By January 1776, George Washington was raising an army, and 260 of its men would come from Barnstable County.

With its expansive coastline, Cape Cod became a major player in the role of our country's defense and one of its largest regiments encompassed Falmouth, Sandwich, Barnstable, and Yarmouth. A French and Indian War veteran from Falmouth, Joseph Dimmick, was appointed the Lieutenant Colonel to oversee this huge contingent. Dimmick was sent out with a sufficient force to patrol the islands around Cape Cod and arrest anyone who might be supplying the enemy with provisions.

A few months later, the Battle of Bunker Hill was fought, and the tide of war quickly drifted to the very door of the Cape. On July 4, 1776, the Declaration of Independence was signed and the residents of Cape Cod wholeheartedly pledged their support in the form of their property and lives. Battle followed battle, and British ships began plying the waters of Buzzards Bay, making it clear that the coastline south of Boston Harbor had to be heavily protected.

Sixty whaleboats were purchased and delivered to Falmouth Harbor, where militia was training to defend this strategic position on the southern side of the Cape. For a year, the British captured ships in and around Falmouth, ransacking them and confiscating their supplies, but in September 1778, Colonel Joseph Dimmick had had enough.

While training the Falmouth militia on the village green, Dimmick rallied some men and took three whaleboats out against the British navy, which resulted in winning back a schooner that had earlier been seized. Many consider this to be the first naval victory in American history, but it would be a few years before the British Royal Navy would admit they had underestimated the vigor and vigilance of the Continental navy. Joseph Dimmick was the key player in this triumph, but it was the events of April 3, 1779, that he would be best remembered for.

On April 2, 1779, Dimmick received word of an imminent attack on Falmouth. The British were coming to burn the town and capture Woods Hole. The militia was alerted, and more than 200 men made their way to Falmouth in less than a day. They dug themselves into trenches along the shore of what is now Surf Drive and waited for the British to arrive.

The next morning, as the fog lifted off the waters of Falmouth Harbor, the troops saw ten British vessels anchored and ready to lay waste to the town. The ships bombarded Falmouth for five and a half hours, with intentions of coming ashore to loot the town of its supplies and weaponry, but Dimmick and his volunteer militia never budged. The British attempted several times to make landfall, but were repelled by the 200 brave Falmouth patriots. King George's ships eventually pulled out and vented their frustration on Nantucket Island. Though not a pivotal moment in the Revolutionary War, it showed the colonists' clear resolve to win their freedom.

JEREMIAH'S GUTTER

- 1804 -

EVERYONE KNOWS THAT YOU AREN'T ON CAPE COD until you cross over the world-famous canal, but what many aren't aware of is that this was not the first man-made waterway dug across the peninsula. More than 200 years before the Cape Cod Canal opened, many of the region's earliest explorers, including Bartholomew Gosnold and the Pilgrims, recognized the need for a passage between the bay and the bodies of water outside the Cape. They had the vision, but not the technology to make it happen. So for another century, sailors and explorers continued to navigate the treacherous shoals around the outer Cape.

For hundreds of years, salt water flooded into the marshy regions around present-day Orleans, particularly during seasonal high tides. Several streams trickling eastward from Cape Cod Bay met the waters of the Atlantic in Nauset Harbor, creating a shallow, natural waterway that allowed small boats to pass between the bay and the ocean. This now forgotten passage ran through the property of Jeremiah

Smith, along the border of what is now Orleans and Eastham. Historians call it "Jeremiah's Drain," but locals used a more colorful name, referring to the old ditch as "Jeremiah's Gutter."

It made sense that as Cape Cod's population and commerce grew, the need for some sort of shortcut out of the bay was essential. The journey from Provincetown to the south side of the Cape was treacherous, especially near the shoals off Truro, and the trip was quite lengthy. Near the elbow of the Cape, a low-lying ridge of land separated Cape Cod Bay from the Atlantic Ocean, and during very high tides the water from the bay would overflow across this swampland, completely isolating the northern part of the Cape. It may have been this type of flooding that, in 1602, had given Bartholomew Gosnold the false impression that Cape Cod was an island.

In the spring of 1717, the folks of Eastham came up with the idea of deepening the natural 1½-mile channel that ran across Jeremiah Smith's land. The hand-dug passage, which connected Boat Meadow Creek on the bay side to Town Cove on the Atlantic side, soon became known as Jeremiah's Gutter. As the name suggests, this channel was very narrow and more akin to a creek than a canal. Boat traffic was subject to the whims of Mother Nature, but when tides and sandbars cooperated, Jeremiah's Gutter could accommodate boats up to twenty tons. This convenient waterway also cut shipping time around the Lower Cape by a full day.

Not long after the ditch was widened, it was put to good use when one of King George's privateers was sent to retrieve the treasure from the wreck of the famous pirate ship, *Whydah*. Captain Cyprian Southack sailed his boats to the wreck site by proceeding from Boston through Cape Cod Bay, and out to the Atlantic via Jeremiah's Gutter. Despite the new shortcut, Southack was unable to get his hands on any gold.

When Orleans broke away from Eastham in 1797, Jeremiah's Gutter formed the northern boundary of the new town. In 1804 the canal was widened and further improved, allowing this humble waterway to play an important role during the War of 1812. As British warships blockaded Cape Cod Bay, local sailors used whaleboats to transport much-needed supplies through the narrow canal, between the bay and the Atlantic. British warships were unable to sail near Orleans because of the shoals, thus making it impossible for the British to gain control of this small, but vital, passage.

In 1865, Henry David Thoreau briefly mentioned the canal in his book titled *Cape Cod*. As he and a friend trekked through the region, he commented on the difficulty they had passing over the waterlogged lands around Orleans. Thoreau also confirmed the importance sailors placed on this (or any) passage through the Cape, by noting that even the smallest channel was important, and was usually dignified with a name—even if it was just a ditch full of water.

By the late 1800s, plans for the new Cape Cod Canal were underway and the use of Jeremiah's Gutter was in decline. A few proposals suggested it be turned into a toll waterway, but those plans never came to fruition. Even if the canal was larger, the wide tidal flats in Cape Cod Bay created problems for big ships, while the shoals and sandbars off Chatham caused problems for everyone. Unfortunately, Jeremiah's Gutter was in an impractical location, and it subsequently fell into disrepair and filled in with silt.

The only evidence that remains of Cape Cod's first canal is its namesake streets, Canal Road and Smith Lane, both of which are located just off the Eastham/Orleans rotary near Route 6. When you are wandering around the shops near Town Cove, or the next time you drive from Orleans into Eastham on Bridge Road, remember that you are on the site of Cape Cod's original canal, Jeremiah's Gutter.

CRANBERRY FEVER

- 1810 -

FROM THE PILGRIMS' THANKSGIVING TABLE to Ocean Spray's bottled fruit juice, the cranberry has become synonymous with Cape Cod. In 1620, when the English colonists first arrived in Massachusetts, they found an abundance of wild, garnet-colored berries all around Cape Cod Bay, and named them "craneberries," because of the pink blossoms that resembled the head and bill of a sandhill crane.

While the settlers named the fruit and recognized it as a valuable bartering item, the Native Americans were the first to make extensive use of this versatile berry. Cranberries served as a healing agent for wounds, were used to dye woven material, and were mashed in with deer meat to make a jerky-type food that could be stored for a very long time. Nowadays, we take for granted all the different forms the cranberry comes in, but it is still one of only three native North American berries that are commercially grown in the United States. Cranberries can be found throughout many of the northern states, but their cultivation began around 1810 in Dennis, Massachusetts.

Cape Cod's ecosystem has never been conducive to conventional farming, which is why the Pilgrims chose not to settle there in the first place, but wild cranberries (along with turnips and asparagus) thrive in the Cape's sandy peats. Cranberries require very odd conditions to grow. They do best in shallow "bowls of land" filled with sand and water, but do not grow consistently from year to year when left to their own devices. By 1800, many locals had laid claim to their own personal "cranberry yards," from which they would harvest a supply of the berries for the winter. But the yield varied dramatically depending on environmental factors. It was far from a reliable crop.

In 1810, Revolutionary War veteran Captain Henry Hall was working on his farm in North Dennis. While clearing some land near the beach, he came upon a patch of cranberry vines that had been covered by windblown sand, and he noticed that rather than dying off, the vines seemed to be thriving. A light bulb went off and Captain Hall transplanted several vines into a fenced area, purposefully spreading sand over them. Come springtime, the vines were flourishing, and by autumn, they produced many more berries that were bigger than ever.

Captain Hall's somewhat fortuitous discovery, keen observation, and intuitive experimentation led to his becoming the first person to successfully cultivate cranberries. It also established the foundation for the local fruit to become a viable commercial crop. It didn't take long for word of this new sanding technique to spread. Others quickly began to copy Hall's method, including another Dennis resident, Eli Howe, who cultivated his own variety, which he named the "Howe" cranberry.

Throughout the early nineteenth century, the number of growers increased rapidly, and by the late 1840s, the commercial center for growing cranberries shifted to Harwich. It was from several bogs in Dennis and Harwich that the cranberry business would blossom.

This area's ideal soil conditions and extended growing season led to further experiments and innovations that paved the way for the large-scale and lucrative cranberry business we know today.

Captain Alvin Cahoon is another one of the industry's earliest pioneers. In 1846, he planted "8 rods to berries" in the Pleasant Lake district of Harwich, creating the country's first commercial cranberry bog. The following year, his cousin, Cyrus Cahoon, also began cultivating cranberries at Pleasant Lake. Innovation must have run in the Cahoon family. Cyrus revolutionized the industry by building the first level-floored cranberry bog, which is still in production more than 150 years later. He also developed the "Early Black" variety of a deep red (almost black) berry that his wife discovered at Black Pond in Harwich. Today, the "Early Black" and "Howe" varieties comprise 95 percent of the cultivars grown in Massachusetts.

Throughout the 1850s and '60s, the cranberry industry flourished due to a combination of successful cultivation techniques and outside economic forces. But it was not yet the cash crop it was hoped to be. For thirty years cranberry farming remained more of a supplement to Cape Cod's other agricultural and maritime commerce—and then it happened! "Cranberry Fever" struck in the middle of the nineteenth century, and it couldn't have come at a better time.

The decades after the Civil War were very depressing, as the bottom fell out of Cape Cod's two major industries—fishing and shipbuilding. Iron steamships replaced the wooden boats built on the Cape, while fish from the West Coast, the Great Lakes, and other inland water sources became more accessible because of the new railroads. The final blow to Cape Cod's economy came during the late 1800s, when the whaling industry all but disappeared. New forms of lighting were being developed and there was no longer a need for whale oil.

A lot of unemployed and retired fishermen and sea captains now needed supplemental income for their families. Those who owned marshy land looked to the berry as their new livelihood. Luckily, as the number of Cape Cod's cranberry growers continued to rise, so did consumer demand. Five acres of cranberry bogs provided a very comfortable living for a farmer, but he and his family could live the high life with ten acres. By 1871, the American Cranberry Grower's Association was formed.

When new manufacturing processes made white sugar available for everyday use, the naturally tart cranberry was sweetened and it became very popular in sauces and other recipes. In the 1930s Ocean Spray began bottling fruit juices, and by the 1960s, the Cape Codder— a mixture of vodka and cranberry—became one of the most popular mixed drinks in history.

Today American farmers harvest approximately 43,000 acres of cranberries each year, with almost half coming from Cape Cod. As the leading agricultural product of Massachusetts, the cranberry remains essential in the ongoing development of Cape Cod. Each September the flaming red fruits of the cranberry bogs are celebrated at Harwich's Cranberry Festival.

THE BATTLE OF ROCK HARBOR

- 1814 -

CAPE COD WAS PARTICULARLY VULNERABLE DURING the War of 1812 and took part in a great number of naval conflicts. Rock Harbor, located on the west side of Orleans, is a relatively narrow and shallow inlet that serves as the town's gateway into Cape Cod Bay. This tranquil cove was the site of a skirmish between locals and the British navy on December 19, 1814.

The United States declared war on Great Britain on June 10, 1812, because U.S. sovereignty had been violated in ways that suggested the new nation was still a colony subject to Britain's imperial whims. Residents of Cape Cod, knowing well the negative effects war would have on the maritime industry, were not particularly supportive. Despite the American government's embargoes against England, much illicit business was carried on between American traders and British officers. Eventually, the United States government was driven to enforce laws prohibiting all trade with Britain.

When the war began, the British government initially enforced a state of blockade only around the Delaware and Chesapeake regions. Great Britain very much needed American supplies for its army in Spain, and Cape Codders wanted to maintain their livelihoods, so both sides remained willing to trade with one another in some capacity. As the war evolved, however, the blockade was extended along the south coast, and then, by May 1814, to the whole east coast, including Cape Cod.

In 1813, a few individuals from the town of Orleans had laid out a road leading to Rock Harbor on Cape Cod Bay, where they built a protected landing place for boats. These individuals originally claimed the land as their personal property, but written deeds or titles could not be produced. Rock Harbor was eventually deemed to be the legal property of the town, and Orleans agreed to pay the expenses for the training of a militia to protect the area, which was highly patrolled by British ships.

By 1814, the size and strength of England's Royal Navy allowed it to blockade all of the ports around Cape Cod Bay, from Provincetown Harbor to Falmouth. American ships that were caught running supplies or trading goods were seized and its crewmembers were taken prisoner. The British ships of war raided the Cape's harbors, sometimes indiscriminately, and burned boats at will. Threats of bombardment and destruction caused the people of Cape Cod to become very vigilant of the British vessels hovering around their shores.

Orleans appointed a committee of safety, and guards were placed on the west shore to sound an alarm if the enemy should attempt to carry out their repeated threats. As an added safety measure, the townspeople who were not formally involved in the militia proposed that they organize an artillery company in case their forces were called to duty in another town. A representative was sent to Boston to request the government supply them with proper weapons, but he was refused and returned to Orleans without munitions. British landing parties began making good on their threats. They ravaged the countryside, stealing crops and livestock, and threatened to destroy the saltworks and other property in the towns. Some of the less scrupulous British commanders demanded payment from the towns-people in exchange for not attacking them. Lord George Stuart, captain of the HMS *Newcastle,* was one of them.

The *Newcastle,* which was part of a squadron led by Commodore George Collier, captured American privateers and harassed the coastal towns of Cape Cod Bay. The British demanded that the town of Orleans ante up a hefty sum of $1,000 for the safety of its citizens; otherwise the town would be bombed and the local saltworks destroyed. The neighboring towns of Eastham and Brewster had already paid handsomely to save their saltworks, but Orleans refused the insulting proposition.

Fortunately for Orleans, the heavily armed ship-of-war was too large to enter the harbor and navigate the marshy Rock Harbor Creek. Several barges full of British soldiers were sent ashore, but the harbor's watchful guards had sufficient time to alert the militia. Men quickly arrived from Orleans and the neighboring towns. After a short skirmish, the militia drove the enemy back to their ship, with only one British casualty.

Not content with the outcome of the failed landing, the *Newcastle* began to fire its cannons, but the ship was too far offshore and the cannonballs fell short. Unable to come any closer to Orleans, the *Newcastle* gave up and went on its way. Five days later, on Christmas Eve, 1814, the Treaty of Ghent was signed and the War of 1812 was over. The large and powerful *Newcastle* lived out a much more mundane career and was eventually disassembled and sold for scrap in 1850.

Orleans led a peaceful existence until another attack occurred one hundred years later, during World War I—only this time the action took place on the Atlantic side of the town. When driving along Route 6 through Orleans, history buffs will appreciate a quick detour into quaint Rock Harbor. No physical evidence exists of the battle, yet one can easily imagine the intimidating ships-of-war hovering along the coastline, and the earliest Americans standing their ground. Nowadays, tranquil Rock Harbor is known for its chartered fishing and breathtaking sunsets.

FALMOUTH UNDER FIRE

- 1814 -

THE AMERICAN REVOLUTION WAS BARELY OVER and the country was pulling itself up by its bootstraps when, in 1803, the aggressive policies of Napoleon Bonaparte pitted two major European powers against one another: England and France. The United States was one of the few countries that preserved its neutrality and remained at peace with the two nations, allowing an unprecedented flourishing of commerce, particularly on Cape Cod, due to its seafaring business.

Unfortunately, this prosperity wasn't to be enjoyed by the citizens of the United States for long. In 1806, Napoleon declared all British islands in a state of blockade, and all commerce and correspondence with the country was prohibited. Consequently, the maritime trade the United States had with England was at a risk of seizure. American commerce would receive another damaging blow when the British government retaliated and stated that all neutral vessels trading with France would be confiscated. In 1807, the British toughened their stance, prohibiting all trade and correspondence with any nation with which England was at war.

In response the United States government, under President Thomas Jefferson, placed an embargo on all exports from the United States to these two countries. The embargo became very unpopular with Americans and was disastrous to the maritime interests of the country. Few suffered more than the people of Cape Cod, who were dependent on trade with Europe and the West Indies for their very existence.

The embargo was repealed by Congress in 1809, only to be followed by another even more restrictive act completely prohibiting all trade with France and England. This strict law was ineffective in forcing the British and French governments to change their position on confiscating American ships, which was becoming fatal to coastal commerce. It was just a matter of time before America would declare war against France or England, or both—but which would it be? The persistent interception of American ships by the British made the decision an obvious one. President James Madison declared war against England on June 10, 1812, thus commencing the War of 1812.

The residents of Cape Cod were not eager for this war, but they knew it was necessary and unavoidable. Local militias, which had not seen action since the Revolutionary War, were called to defend their towns as best they could. Once the news reached England that war had been declared, British ships began to assemble up and down the New England coast, and its towns were soon under attack. Massachusetts Bay came entirely under control of the British early in the war, thwarting communication between Boston and other commercial ports.

British men-of-war began cruising the bays throughout Cape Cod, raiding harbors and burning all boats that attempted to run supplies or trade goods. No part of the state was more harassed than the towns of Barnstable County—Falmouth in particular.

Falmouth's strategic location on the southern side of the Cape allowed the Falmouth Artillery Company to fire regularly on British ships. In turn, Falmouth was under almost constant attack by the Royal Navy. Some Cape Cod towns, such as Brewster and Eastham, paid a handsome price to British commanders to avoid being bombed or ransacked, but Falmouth refused to sell out.

The HMS *Nimrod*, a British sloop of war, sailed into the waters of New England in 1813. This fast, well-built ship was named for an Old Testament hunter, and the symbolism was not lost on the religious folk of Cape Cod. It was part of a squadron sent to seek out and destroy American privateers. The *Nimrod*, under the command of Captain Nathaniel Mitchell, began preying on boats around Cape Cod. By October 1813, it was the scourge of Buzzards Bay.

In January 1814, a squadron of British ships, including the *Nimrod*, set up a command post at Tarpaulin Cove in the Elizabeth Islands. They used an inn, well known among local mariners, as headquarters. On the eve of January 13, 1814, the innkeeper overheard the crew of the *Nimrod* planning an attack on Falmouth. They wanted the city's brass cannons, which were becoming quite a nuisance to the British ships cruising the Cape's southern shoreline. The innkeeper had sufficient time to warn the town, where the militia was already well dug in.

On the morning of January 28, 1814, the *Nimrod* sailed into Falmouth Harbor and dropped anchor. The commander raised a truce flag and sent a small party ashore to demand the town surrender its two cannons and a sloop in the harbor—otherwise, Falmouth would be bombed. Not only was their demand refused, but the commander of the Falmouth Artillery Company, Captain Westin Jenkins, challenged the British, saying, "if ye want the cannon, come and get it!"

Captain Mitchell gave the town until noon to comply, but they had no intentions of doing so. They had just enough time to rally the local militia and remove all the sick, women, children, and furniture to a safer place. An hour later, the Battle of Falmouth commenced.

The *Nimrod* spent the better part of the day unloading more than 300 cannonballs across Falmouth. The gunfire finally subsided at night, but the townspeople were uncertain what fate awaited them in the morning. Surprisingly, at sunrise, the *Nimrod* pulled up anchor and sailed westward to meet up with another ship-of-war back at Tarpaulin Cove.

Fortunately, no one was killed or even injured, but several of Falmouth's buildings sustained considerable damage. In fact, a few still show the scars of cannonball fire, including the Elm Arch Inn, built in 1810, as well as the appropriately named restaurant, "The Nimrod." (Its cannonball hole is located in the men's room.)

On June 13, 1814, the *Nimrod* ingloriously ran aground after successfully attacking and burning seventeen ships in Buzzards Bay. The crew frantically dumped several of its cannons overboard, lightening the load until it was able to sail away. In 1987, divers recovered five cannons from the waters of Buzzards Bay. One of these cannons can be seen at the Falmouth Historical Society, which amusingly declares the "British never got our cannons, but we got one of theirs."

TWIST OF FATE

- 1815 -

HISTORIANS ARE FULL OF "WHAT IFS." What if, after the Battle of Waterloo, Napoleon Bonaparte escaped to America rather than surrendering to the English? Would he have taken up residence on Cape Cod—or in New Jersey, where his brother, Joseph Bonaparte, had emigrated? Though it's just a matter of speculation now, Captain Jeremiah Mayo could have changed the course of history by carrying out plans to bring Napoleon to America in 1815.

Mayo was born in Brewster on January 29, 1786. He was the son of a blacksmith but developed a taste for life at sea after spending the summer following his fourteenth birthday fishing at the Straits of Belle Isle in Newfoundland. By the age of eighteen, he convinced his reluctant father to let him sail to the Bahamas for a load of salt. How does a father argue with a son who is articulate, headstrong, and 6 feet, 4 inches tall? This marked the beginning of what would be many trips to the Caribbean and Europe, particularly to French ports.

Mayo made his first voyage to the southern French city of Marseilles in 1804—the same year Napoleon Bonaparte proclaimed himself emperor and sold the Louisiana Territory to the Americans. During the next few years, while sailing around the Mediterranean, Mayo visited many places associated with the Bonapartes in one way or another. His ships carried cargoes of fish, flour, cider, and wine to and from the ports of Malaga, San Sebastian; Gibraltar, Spain; Lisbon, Portugal; and even as far north as Amsterdam.

Bordeaux, on the southwest coast of France, was a region Captain Mayo frequented to replenish his cargo of wine. It was during an 1808 visit to Bayonne that he encountered the legendary Napoleon on horseback, rallying his army to invade Spain. But Mayo's high regard for the emperor was not necessarily the consensus. Thomas Jefferson, for instance, believed Napoleon to be a tyrannical monster who was unduly admired. Still, the post–Revolutionary War sentiment was such that many Americans still felt a great contempt for the British and often embraced the enemies of England as friends of the United States—including Napoleon, dictator or not.

Having had his own ship come under attack several times in the Mediterranean, and being under constant threat of seizure by the British warships in the Atlantic, Mayo's admiration of Napoleon's military prowess is understandable. Also, the French were at war with a country that was seizing American ships and hurting Cape Cod's maritime trade. The British hitting so close to home may have been another reason Captain Mayo appreciated Napoleon's efforts.

In the early months of 1809, Mayo made his way back to his farm in Brewster, where he married Sally Crosby. He spent the next two years sticking close to home and was one of ten delegates selected to represent his hometown at meetings about another potential war with Great Britain. Once the War of 1812 broke out, Mayo was back to running cargo across the Atlantic.

Captain Mayo made several trips to Sweden, Germany, Belgium, and even England in his newly built ship, the *Sally*. He managed to out-maneuver British sloops with his fast brig, and he regularly brought European goods back to Boston and Cape Cod. He was well known for his uncanny navigational skills and keen judgment. While in command of his ships, he never lost a man nor suffered a wreck—even when the New England harbors were chock-full of enemy warships. His reputation preceded him everywhere he went.

While America was standing its ground during the war with Great Britain, Napoleon was losing his. On April 12, 1814, he unconditionally abdicated the throne and was sent into exile on the Italian island of Elba. It took less than ten months for him to plot his escape, and by March 1, 1815, he was back in France, marching to Paris. For one hundred days Napoleon was once again the ruler of France, but the rest of Europe was not going to let it be without a fight.

In June, Napoleon led his troops into Belgium, where they battered the Prussian Army. However, the British Army at Waterloo proved to be too much. On June 18, 1815, British and Prussian troops came together under the command of the Duke of Wellington and defeated Napoleon's forces at the famous Battle of Waterloo. In the weeks following his second abdication, Napoleon went back to Paris to figure out what to do next. He discussed the idea of seeking refuge in the United States with one of his aides.

A few weeks after the battle, Captain Mayo happened to be in France. He docked the *Sally* in the port at Havre on the northwestern coast, conveniently close to Paris. Was he there for more wine? Or was he aware that he was going to be interviewed by an agent of Napoleon Bonaparte? Knowing Mayo's reputation for avoiding the British fleet, an aide sought out the captain to inquire if he would smuggle the emperor to the United States. Everyone understood what a dangerous undertaking this would be. If the ship was captured or searched, it would result in the confiscation of the vessel and, more importantly, its precious cargo, but Mayo consented.

A French paper dated June 30, 1815, claims that Napoleon left Paris with six carriages, en route to the west coast. According to the article, he was attempting to flee the country. It also stated that a large American ship was awaiting his arrival. Could it have been the *Sally*? That same month the emperor's brother wrote a letter to his sister, stating that Napoleon "will depart for the United States . . . where all of us will join him."

The British caught wind of Napoleon's plan and sent ships to blockade French ports up and down the coast. They also searched as many ships as possible before allowing them to sail away. A popular story claims that Napoleon held Emmanuel Courvoisier's cognac in such high esteem that he stocked a ship full of barrels to take with him. This ship was seized, but when officers sampled the brandy, they were so impressed that they referred to it as *le Cognac de Napoleon.* The term Napoleon Cognac stuck.

Neither the cognac nor the emperor made it to the United States. On July 17, 1815, Napoleon had the misfortune of being intercepted by the British in Rochefort, France, where the American ship was supposedly waiting for him. Rather than attempt to flee, Napoleon decided that, as a general and a monarch, he could not abandon the soldiers who supported him, and he gave himself up. Soon afterward, Captain Mayo heard that Napoleon had surrendered himself to the British, and he returned to Cape Cod without his intended cargo. It is presumed that had Napoleon followed through with this escape, he would have made it safely to America, as Jeremiah Mayo sailed the *Sally* from France to Boston without encountering the British.

Napoleon was not given asylum in England as expected but was quickly deported to the prison island of St. Helena, where he lived the remainder of his life in exile. Though the disgraced emperor did not end up in America for his "retirement," some of the Bonaparte family did. His elder brother Joseph settled in Bordentown, New Jersey, and bought land in upstate New York, where Lake Bonaparte is a reminder of what could have been. Napoleon realized the mistake he had made in a letter written to his sister. He expressed his regret over not being smuggled to America, and on January 17, 1816, he began taking English lessons. It was supposedly to read what the English papers were saying about him, but who knows? Perhaps Napoleon was planning another great escape.

Captain Mayo resigned from sea life in 1819 to lead the Brewster artillery company, and then became the president of Brewster Marine Insurance Company. In 1881, a friend wrote that General Mayo was "a man who had seen a great deal of the world and had rare conversational powers to tell stories that created pictures of places and scenes." One is left to wonder how Jeremiah Mayo told the story of planning Napoleon's escape to America and whether he too speculated, "what if?"

SANDWICH GLASS:
LIGHTING THE WAY

- 1825 -

IN THE MIDDLE OF THE NINETEENTH CENTURY, when many of the Cape towns were becoming famous for maritime industries and beaches, the town of Sandwich was gaining international recognition as a center for glassmaking. In 1825, the distinguished and colorful entrepreneur Deming Jarves was lured from Boston's New England Glass Company to establish the Sandwich Glass Manufactory on Cape Cod.

He chose the Sandwich area, not so much for its sand (an essential ingredient in the making of glass) but for the abundance of timber, which could be used to fuel the furnaces. He also knew Sandwich's coastal location would come in handy when it came time to ship the goods. The following year, the business was incorporated as the Boston and Sandwich Glass Company. It met with instant success, but few envisioned just how definitively this company would revolutionize the glassmaking industry.

Jarves was not just an experienced china merchant; he was educated in glass technology and trends, and he was very much ahead of his time. This visionary man had employee housing built around the factory and hired a logging company to clear 2,000 acres of forest for the wood. He even built his own steamship out of frustration with the railroad transportation system and its steep fees. Most importantly, Jarves brought the best glassblowers from around the world to this small village, and in less than a quarter century, Sandwich was the most successful town on the Cape.

At its peak, the company employed more than 500 people. It was the first factory in the country to make pressed glass (also known as lacy glass), and, because of semi-automation, it was the first to have large-scale production. This, combined with the introduction of coal to the industry (furnaces could now be heated 300 degrees higher), allowed for larger, more elaborate patterned pieces to be made.

Highly skilled craftsmen made exquisite objects d'art that bring big bucks at today's auctions, but the glassworkers mostly turned out an endless number of practical objects that were affordable for the average wage earner. The Sandwich Glass Company was the first to manufacture glass tableware, and, with half a ton of glassware being shipped from the Cape each week, it quickly became one of America's largest and best-known glass companies. Despite mass-production, it maintained a reputation for creating high-quality pieces—particularly, lighting devices.

Sandwich Glass's first artisans created glass objects by hand blowing individual pieces. This was the most common and least complicated method of glassmaking, but it was also an extremely time-consuming and costly process. Among the earliest free-blown pieces made at Sandwich were whale oil lamps.

Whale oil lamps are considered an American innovation, but oil-burning lamps have been in use as far back as prehistoric times, when shells and hollowed-out stones acted as reservoirs to burn animal and nut oils. The Greeks replaced handheld torches with terra cotta oil-burning lamps, while the Romans and early medieval artisans elevated lighting devices to an art form. It wasn't until the late eighteenth century, out of need for brighter lighthouse lamps, that advancements in lighting really began to take shape. From that point on, developments happened so fast that they were sometimes obsolete before they even had a chance to catch on.

In 1782, a Swiss scientist, Aimé Argand, designed a smokeless oil-burning lamp that provided seven times the light of one candle. But for the average consumer, most liquid fuels were expensive, messy, and often dangerous. Most households continued to use candles and fireplaces for light well into the mid-1800s, even though candles were smoky and dripped wax everywhere, while burning animal fat and tallow smelled foul. Oil-burning lamps were rare and expensive in early America, but Sandwich Glass played its part in the important, albeit short, history of these specialized lamps.

Cape Cod's whaling industry just happened to be in its heyday when the Sandwich Glass Company was formed. Fishermen discovered that the oil from the heads of sperm whales burned clearer and brighter than most others—and like beeswax, it did not emit a disagreeable odor. One of the world's largest mammals suddenly became the prime target of an already lucrative whale-hunting business. It wasn't long before overfishing drove the cost of whale oil beyond the reach of all but the wealthiest people.

Most families could not afford whale oil; those who could wanted proper lamps to burn their high-quality fuel—yet no efficient burning systems existed. Whale oil tended to thicken as it cooled, so an old burner style was redesigned to keep the wick's flame low to warm the oil, keeping it fluid.

Pairs of whale oil lamps were among the earliest items made when the factory first opened. The production life of these lamps mirrored the whale-hunting industry. They were at their most popular between the 1840s and 1860s, and when the bottom fell out of whaling, the lamps all but disappeared. Sandwich whale oil lamps are now considered by glass collectors to be some of the most beautiful American lamps in existence.

The Sandwich Glass Company might, however, be best known for its candlesticks. Even with oil-burning devices, candlelight remained an important secondary light source, so the factory continually produced candlesticks. With the onset of kerosene burners and electric lighting, candles became less relevant, but still did not fall by the wayside. They became popular for mood lighting, and the form of the candlestick became more decorative.

The most popular Sandwich Glass motif was the dolphin candlestick, which was made in great quantities for about twenty years, between 1850 and 1870. The candlesticks featured the figural dolphin's oversized head resting on the base, while its tail flipped in the air to support the socket for the candle. This design came in a variety of sizes and colors and was copied by factories from Pittsburgh to Czechoslovakia, attesting to its trendiness and appeal. Competition sprung up throughout the Midwest, and glassmakers began producing mass quantities of affordable products, many of which mimicked Sandwich Glass patterns and borrowed its pioneering techniques.

In the 1880s, when the Boston and Sandwich Glass Company was at its creative and technical best, troubles with the growing labor movement and cheaper midwestern options brought the company to a screeching halt. On New Year's Day in 1888, the factory closed its doors. Today, one piece of Sandwich glass could sell for tens of thousands of dollars. If you are unable to form your own collection, you may want to visit the Sandwich Glass Museum. Established in the early 1920s by the Sandwich Historical Society, the museum preserves and showcases more than 5,000 pieces of the rare glass, including many of the whale oil lamps and candlesticks that lit the way for modern glassworks.

THE GREAT FIRE OF NANTUCKET

- 1846 -

BETWEEN THE YEARS OF 1800 AND 1850, Nantucket Town was considered the "Whaling Capital of the World." It was the third-largest city in Massachusetts, behind only Boston and Salem, and was one of the wealthiest communities in the country—but all this changed in just seven hours. On the night of July 13, 1846, the worst fire in Nantucket history raged across town, leveling most of the commercial district, homes, and wharves. By morning nearly forty acres lay in ashes, and hundreds of people were left homeless. This devastating tragedy, now known as the Great Fire, not only destroyed the physical structure of the city, but also wiped out the infrastructure of the entire whaling industry.

Prior to the Great Fire, Nantucket Town had experienced a number of conflagrations, including two devastating blazes very close together—one in 1836 and another in 1838. As a result of these fires, the Nantucket Fire Department was established. Because most of the buildings in the business district were constructed of wood, the downtown area was a complete fire hazard. Fire safety was a primary concern, but little could be done to fireproof the city.

Even during the zenith of prosperity, the only brick buildings in Nantucket Town were the Old Town Building on Union Street and the Rotch Market on Main Street. Everything in between was made of wood, including most residential properties. As whaling merchants and ship captains began to gain unprecedented wealth, however, they showcased their economic and social status by building new, opulent homes.

In 1829, Jared Coffin, a prosperous shipbuilder, commissioned Nantucket's very first brick residence at 19 Pleasant Street. Shortly thereafter, other local "oil barons" felt obliged to keep up with the Joneses. Elegant brick houses sprung up quickly throughout the neighborhood. Members of the Coffin clan built homes at 75 and 78 Main Street, while Joseph Starbuck built three matching residences for his sons, just seven doors down. In 1845, Starbuck's large, stylish house on New Dollar Lane prompted Jared Coffin to build an even more extravagant home (presently the Coffin House Inn), at 29 Broad Street.

Unbeknownst to them, this competitive display of wealth would help curtail the Great Fire that roared through Nantucket Town just a year after Coffin built his second home. Not only would these stalwart structures withstand the flames, their brick walls, slate roofs, and cobblestone pavements would stop the catastrophic blaze from spreading any farther than it did.

Around 11:00 P.M. on July 13, 1846, a stovepipe caught fire in a downtown hat store. Within an hour it was burning out of control. Frantic cries of "Fire! Fire!" echoed through town. Nantucketers poured onto the streets to help fight the fiery inferno that was spreading rapidly from one wooden building to another. The fire department finally arrived with their hand-pumped hose carts, while people scrambled to save whatever they could from their homes and busi-nesses. The streets were cluttered with clothes, furniture, and chil-dren covered protectively in wet blankets, but there wasn't much that could be done.

The wharves were equally doomed. Dozens of whale-oil process-ing factories and storehouses were clustered along the waterfront. As soon as the scorching heat reached the combustible barrels of oil, the highly combustible buildings burst into flames. One eyewitness stated that it was like "a sea of fire," as burning oil spilled out into the water. All anyone could do was stand by and watch the island's wealth go up in flames.

Locals worked particularly hard to save the Nantucket Atheneum Library and Museum. The historically important building hosted a number of the country's most acclaimed speakers: Ralph Waldo Emerson, Henry David Thoreau, John James Audubon, and, of par-ticular historical importance, Frederick Douglass, who gave his first major speech here in front of a mixed-race crowd in 1841. It also housed collections of old documents and artifacts related to Nan-tucket's maritime industries, as well as fascinating objects brought back by whalers from their journeys around the world. Valiant attempts were made to remove books, paintings, and sculpted busts from the Library Room, but to no avail. The fire was just too pow-erful, and very little was rescued.

By early morning, the Great Fire had consumed everything from the Rotch Market to the Pacific National Bank on Main Street. The blaze was stopped at Pearl Street (modern-day India Street), but not before destroying more than 250 buildings—including all of the town's markets, shops, seven whale oil factories, twelve warehouses, and three of the four wharfs. One-third of the community had been burnt to the ground. In terms of today's dollars, an estimated $24 million in damage was done.

Within days officials made a heartfelt plea for aid, after which donations of money, food, and clothing poured in for the 800 people left homeless and jobless. Within weeks reconstruction efforts were underway. It took the industrious and tenacious Nantucketers only a few months to rebuild the business district.

With an added emphasis on fire prevention, fourteen new commercial buildings and most of the new shops were constructed entirely of brick. Additional fire-prevention measures were implemented by building several hose-cart houses in which to store fire-fighting apparatus. One of these firehouses, located at 8 Gardner Street, currently exhibits rare fire-fighting equipment and information about the Great Fire.

In less than two years, a new and fireproof town rose from the ashes, but the whaling industry wasn't as fortunate. The Great Fire destroyed all that was essential to the island's commerce: warehouses, ropewalks, wharves, and oil-processing and candle-making factories. The fire, however, was just one of several factors that brought about the quick downfall of the whaling industry and Nantucket's economy.

Shifting sandbars and the silting up of harbors made it difficult for the increasingly large whaling boats to dock in Nantucket. The California Gold Rush enticed seafaring adventurers to seek their wealth in the foothills of the Sierra Nevada. The final blow to the whaling industry came in 1859, with the discovery of petroleum, a cheaper form of fuel. Nantucket's glory days were over by the start of the Civil War.

Today, you can be transported back to Nantucket's Golden Age at the Whaling Museum, presently located in one of the spermaceti candle factories constructed just after the Great Fire. Also, because of excellent rebuilding and preservation efforts, more than 800 pre–Civil War houses remain standing on Nantucket. The island now has more totally preserved buildings on the National Registry of Historic Places than anywhere in Massachusetts—including Boston, Plymouth, and Salem.

CAPTAIN EDWARD PENNIMAN'S
WHALE OF A HOME

- 1868 -

THE REMARKABLY PRESERVED VICTORIAN HOME of Edward Penniman overlooks the Atlantic Ocean from atop Fort Hill in Eastham. It stands as a tribute to the extraordinary life of one of the most successful whaling captains in New England. This wealthy, worldly Cape Codder made a fortune traveling the world in pursuit of the creatures of the deep. By age fifty-three, Captain Penniman had accumulated enough riches to retire anywhere in the world, but chose his beloved Eastham as the site for building an opulent mansion for his family. The Penniman House is now a historic site that tells the true-life story of a man who traversed the globe in pursuit of whaling—while in his heart, he was never far from Cape Cod.

Edward Penniman believed there was no lovelier place on earth than Eastham, the town in which he was born on August 16, 1831. Most Cape Cod fishermen had an early start to life at sea, and Edward was no different. At age eleven he was fishing off the coast of

Newfoundland, Canada; at twenty-one, he went on his first whaling expedition. Soon after, he became the captain of his own ship and chose the mainland port of New Bedford as home base. It was from New Bedford that he launched seven whale hunts, which took him around the world for years at a time. He entered ports as far-flung as the Arctic, the Cape Verde Islands, New Zealand, and Hawaii.

Penniman was fascinated with foreign cultures and collected countless souvenirs during his journeys, but letters home often hinted that he preferred life on land to being at sea. Edward missed his family, but given his penchant for adventure and his taste for the finer things in life, he could not ignore the extreme wealth attainable through whaling.

The Pennimans eventually decided to make the best of Edward's career choice and turned several of the whaling expeditions into family affairs. Having his wife and children accompany him for three or four years made the voyages much more tolerable. In fact, his wife, Betsy Augusta Penniman (whom he called "Gustie"), actually enjoyed life aboard the ship. She wrote in her memoirs that she enjoyed cooking and sewing, corresponding with friends back home, and even developing her navigational skills.

Their children also accompanied the Pennimans on three of the whale hunts. A voyage to the Arctic Ocean inspired their first son, Eugene, to follow in his father's footsteps and become a whaling ship captain. The Pennimans' youngest child, Neddie, went along on the second trip and entertained himself during the three-year journey by modeling wooden boats and sketching ships. The third and final trip included their thirteen-year-old daughter, Bessie, who had the opportunity to meet the Hawaiian royal family, and who enjoyed sailing through warmer climates, such as Panama, San Francisco, and Hawaii.

In the 1860s the going rates for whale oil varied from $1.45 to $2.55 per gallon, while whalebone sold for $15.80 per pound.

Records indicate Penniman's ships carried thousands of barrels of whale oil and more than a hundred-thousand pounds of whalebone. Do the math and it's easy to see how he amassed such a fortune. Captain Penniman became so successful in the whaling industry, or "whale fishery" as it was called, that he earned enough money to put his family in the lap of luxury—despite his distaste for life at sea.

So, what should he do with all this money? Build a house!

In 1868, after his fourth whaling expedition, Penniman returned to Eastham, purchased twelve acres of land from his father, and constructed an impressive home for himself and his family. He chose a site located on the west side of Town Cove, in the Fort Hill section of Eastham. This very narrow neck of Cape Cod is only about 3 miles wide from the Atlantic Ocean to Cape Cod Bay, and like any whaler of his time, Edward couldn't bear to be far from the sea, so he built his grand house on a cliff overlooking the Atlantic.

Most of the conservative Eastham residents lived in simple Cape Cod homes, but the worldly Pennimans had no qualms about building a modern, over-the-top mansion to showcase their treasures from around the globe. Well-versed in the most up-to-date trends, Penniman constructed his impressive home in the French Second Empire style.

This sophisticated style, inspired by Napoleon III, was highly ornamental and included many of the architectural features, such as mansard roofs, that one might see while strolling along the grand boulevards of Paris. Closely associated with the prosperous administration under President Ulysses S. Grant (1860–1877), it is sometimes referred to as the General Grant Style.

The Pennimans' two-and-a-half-story wood frame house has a steeply pitched mansard roof that looks like it came straight from the movie *Psycho*. The house is clapboard-covered and painted in a lively rainbow of colors: yellow siding, white trim, black windows, green blinds, and brown and red roof shingles. It must have been quite a site to their puritanical neighbors!

Captain Penniman spared no expense in building the most extravagant and modern house in Eastham, and possibly on the Cape. It wasn't, however, the size or its ornate details and elevated location that distinguished it from the simple homes of Cape Cod. The Penniman House was most impressively on the cutting edge of home technology.

It was the first in Eastham to have indoor plumbing, using the most contemporary techniques available at the time. A rooftop collection system gathered water into a cistern in the attic. Gravity drew the water from this tank down through pipes leading into the kitchen and bathroom. The heating and lighting systems of the home were also updated as new technology was developed. They evolved from using wood and coal fuel to kerosene and, eventually, electricity.

Inside and out, this unique house reveals how wealthy whaling families lived in the nineteenth century, and reflects the tastes they had developed after a lifetime of exposure to so many different world cultures. The rooms of the Penniman House were filled with imagination-stirring collections of artifacts, ranging from Arctic bear robes to European paintings to Nantucket scrimshaw.

Most symbolic of Edward Penniman's livelihood is the thirteen-foot whale jawbone that frames an entrance to the property, acting as a gateway. Passing between the whale bones is believed to bring good luck—and there is no doubt that Edward Penniman had a little bit of this in his lifetime. At age fifty-three, he retired as one of the most successful whaling captains in New England history.

In 1884, Edward was finally able to sit back and enjoy the fruits of his labors. He returned permanently to his beloved Fort Hill and his grand home. More than a century later, the Penniman House remains in a remarkable state of preservation. The floor plan is the same as it was in 1868, and most of the interior woodwork, finishes, hardware, and wall and ceiling coverings are original.

In recognition of the home's historical significance and its connection with the region's whaling era and this prestigious family, the Cape Cod National Seashore purchased the priceless property from Irma Penniman Broun, the captain's youngest granddaughter, in the 1960s. Today, the Penniman House is a National Historic Site. Exhibitions of the family's written records, personal collections, and more than one hundred glass-plate pictures, taken between 1880 and 1913 by Captain Penniman's daughter Bessie, are on display. These eclectic artifacts offer a glimpse into the Pennimans' fascinating lives— and one of the most historically important homes on Cape Cod.

THE FRENCH CONNECTION

- 1891 -

HAVE YOU EVER WONDERED HOW NEWS made its way around the world before cell phones and instant messaging, satellite dishes and cable television? Very slowly! Before the first transatlantic cable was laid in the late 1900s, word traveled only as fast as the horse or the ship carrying it. Communication between Europe and North America took upwards of a week, but that was considered normal for the time.

It wasn't until 1891 that the two continents were permanently connected via an underwater cable that ran between northern France and Cape Cod. The modest French Cable Station is located off Route 28 in Orleans. It houses the original communication equipment, which may seem primitive in this day and age, but at the turn of the twentieth century, it was state-of-the-art technology.

The precedent for modern communication was set in the 1830s, when Professor Samuel Morse sent a message via Morse code from Baltimore to Washington. Within thirty years, historians recognized his magnetic telegraph as one of the most beneficial and important inventions of mankind. Telegraph lines appeared all over Europe and North America, and messages could be sent virtually instantaneously overland. Crossing water, however, presented a true challenge.

Communication technology was in its infancy when, in 1845, the idea of a transatlantic cable was proposed. Scientists knew the underwater wires had to be heavily insulated and exceedingly strong to withstand the great depths of the Atlantic, but practical demonstrations proved it could be done. In 1851, after several failed attempts, two visionary British brothers, John and Jacob Brett, finally succeeded in running a cable across the English Channel to France.

In 1856, the brothers joined an American named Cyrus Field in forming the Atlantic Telegraph Company, and by June of 1857, 2,500 nautical miles of cable had been manufactured. In August, the monstrous cable was loaded onto two ships and the formidable task of laying the transatlantic cable began. Cyrus Field and his engineers were about to be taught very expensive lessons in trial and error!

Beginning in Valentia Harbor, Ireland, the ships sailed together into the Atlantic while slowly dropping the cable into the ocean. Everything seemed to be going as planned, but six days and 380 miles into the project, a wave crashed into the boat and the cable snapped. The ships were forced to return to port because they did not have enough cable to continue on.

With high hopes and another 700 feet of cable, a new approach was taken for connecting the two continents. On June 25, 1858, the same two ships met each other in the middle of the Atlantic and joined their respective ends of the cable. However, as soon as they began to sail in opposite directions, the cable broke! It continued to snap after the third and fourth attempts, so the engineers cut their losses and returned to Britain.

With just enough cable for one last try, the ships once again met in the mid-Atlantic, and this time successfully laid the cable between

Ireland and Newfoundland, Canada. On August 5, 1858, the two continents were connected—but not for long! In less than a month, the high voltages used to send messages had fried the cables, and communication ceased. It was back to the drawing board! More than two decades would pass before another attempt was made.

In 1879, the Compagnie Française du Télégraphe de Paris à New York was formed, with the sole purpose of laying a transatlantic cable. The company decided the cable should run between Brest, France, to the island of St. Pierre in the Miquelon Islands, then on to Eastham, Cape Cod. Using a cable manufactured in England by the Siemens Brothers and an enormous American ship, the USS *Faraday*, the cable was laid in less than four months. It stretched 2,242 nautical miles across the Atlantic to St. Pierre and continued another 827 nautical miles on to Cape Cod.

A large building was constructed in North Eastham to serve as a cable station for receiving messages from Europe and then transmitting them on to New York, via an overland telegraph line. Interestingly, the cable arrived in Cape Cod two weeks before the station was completed, so it was temporarily housed in the Nauset Beach Light keeper's house, and later transferred.

After a short time, the station workers felt the Nauset location was inconvenient, and the cable company shifted its Cape Cod operation to Orleans, where they built the French Cable Station in March of 1891. A connector cable was laid from the old station at Nauset, across Nauset Marsh, to the new cable station in Orleans.

From this point on, technology advanced rapidly. Within seven years the cable, which came to be known as "Le Direct," totally bypassed Saint-Pierre and ran non-stop between Brittany, France, and Cape Cod, allowing instantaneous, two-way communication across the Atlantic for the first time—and it came in handy! During its heyday, the French Cable Station played a vital role in a number of major international events. Many important messages were conveyed from the Orleans station.

In November 1898, the *Portland*, a steamship with hundreds of passengers aboard, sank in a battering winter storm. With wreckage and bodies washing ashore on Cape Cod, the French Cable Station was the first to transmit news to the world that there were no survivors. It took a mere five minutes for the message to be relayed from Orleans to France then back to New York.

On May 31, 1927, it was befitting that news of another monumental transatlantic event was transmitted from the French Cable Station. From Cape Cod, the nation learned that Charles Lindbergh had made the first solo transatlantic crossing, flying the *Spirit of St. Louis* from New York to Paris.

This humble building also played an important role in both world wars. During World War I, the station was an essential lifeline between army headquarters in Washington, D.C., and the American forces in France. Marines guarded the cable station, which was used to send top-secret messages back and forth between the two countries.

The cable remained in operation throughout World War II, until France surrendered to Germany. In June 1940, an abrupt message arrived in Orleans reading, "Les Boches sont ici" (the Germans are here). Immediately afterward, the cable went dead. The French end of the cable was now in the hands of the Nazis, and both transmitters remained quiet throughout the rest of the war.

The cable hut in Orleans remained vacant long after World War II ended, and despite more than 600 cables being laid around the world, the French Cable Station did not resume transmissions until 1952. This second life, however, was to be short-lived. By the mid-twentieth century, telephone service had rendered the station obsolete, and it was forced to close its doors for good on November 24, 1959.

Inside the station, a faded 1959 calendar still hangs on the wall with November 26 heavily circled in pencil. The final message sent across the cable from Orleans read, "Have a happy Thanksgiving. Station closed," and the telegraph was shut down permanently. The French Cable Station, which once served as a vital communication link between America and Europe stands today near Town Cove in Orleans. The museum displays all the original communication equipment and is open to visitors most weekdays in the summer and weekends in the fall.

CAN YOU HEAR ME NOW?—
THE WIRELESS INDUSTRY IS BORN

- 1903 -

His Majesty, Edward VII.
London, Eng.
In taking advantage of the wonderful triumph of scien-
tific research and ingenuity which has been achieved in
perfecting a system of wireless telegraphy, I extend on
behalf of the American People most cordial greetings
and good wishes to you and to all the people of the
British Empire.

THEODORE ROOSEVELT
Wellfleet, Mass., Jan. 19, 1903

Sandrinham, January 19, 1903
The President,
White House, Washington, America
I thank you most sincerely for the kind message which I
have just received from you, through Marconi's trans-
Atlantic wireless telegraphy. I sincerely reciprocate in
the name of the British Empire the cordial greetings
and friendly sentiment expressed by you on behalf of the
American Nation, I heartily wish you and your coun-
try every possible prosperity.

EDWARD R. and I.

So read the first two-way, transatlantic, wireless telegraph message, tapped out in Morse code between President Theodore Roosevelt and Edward VII, King of England. The technology that allowed this to happen had not been developed by an American but rather by the Irish-Italian–born Guglielmo Marconi. His dream of wireless communication was realized not in his homeland of Italy, but in America, on Cape Cod.

By his own admission Marconi was neither an inventor nor formally educated in the sciences. In fact, he never performed well enough to be accepted to a university. But he did have deep pockets, family connections, and serious entrepreneurial vision. His mother, Annie Marconi, was the daughter of the famed Andrew Jameson, an Irish whiskey baron, and Marconi grew up a persistent and privileged boy, with the finances to support his tireless experimenting with radio frequency.

By 1895, at age twenty-one, Marconi was finally able to piece together several existing bits of technology: a Morse code key, some batteries, an induction coil, a relay, a device for detecting radio waves called a "coherer," and his own personal invention, the aerial and earth. As backyard experiments proved, this contraption could transmit messages via radio frequency as far as one and one-quarter mile—and through a hillside.

Marconi's intuitive vision of wireless communication between two points—through land masses, across water, and despite the curvature of the earth—using his transmitting device led him to do what any loyal Italian would do: offer the technology first to the Italian government. In typical bureaucratic fashion, the government dragged their feet too long, and in 1896 Marconi made his way to England. There, with a little help from family and friends in high places, his dream of sending a wireless signal across the Atlantic to North America would come to fruition.

In some ways, Marconi's lack of formal education contributed to his success. Many scientists disagreed with him that radio waves could work beyond the horizon. With his unstoppable attitude, rather than crunch numbers and debate the skeptics, he set out to prove that his instincts and theories were correct. Through ongoing experiments, Marconi demonstrated over and over that wireless transmission had the potential to compete with the cables that had been laid across the Atlantic. After successfully transmitting messages across the English Channel to France, it was time to attempt the Atlantic.

In 1900, a high-powered transmitting station was built on the south coast of England, in the village of Poldhu in Cornwall. From here, Marconi's team performed successful transmissions between England and Ireland. In 1901 Cape Cod was identified as the place to build the first wireless station in America.

After being denied the opportunity to build near the Highland Light at Truro, and passing up permission to build in the Barnstable area, Marconi settled on South Wellfleet. This area was chosen for its elevated table of land overlooking the ocean. As Henry David Thoreau once described it, it is a place "where a man may stand . . . and put all of America behind him." Wellfleet, located on the "wrist" of the Cape, was a likely and philosophical choice.

Headquarters were set up in the Holbrook House in Wellfleet, and Marconi's men went to work building the towers. Despite storms toppling the aerials in Poldhu and a nor'easter blowing over the unsafe aerials in Cape Cod, Marconi persisted. The station in South Wellfleet was rebuilt with a better design and a transmitter building with a buzz that could be heard 3 miles away—but the 20,000-volt transformer wasn't the only buzz around town.

Recognizing the potential for profit in a radio link between North America and Britain, Marconi wanted publicity for his new technology. He convinced President Theodore Roosevelt to come to the station at South Wellfleet on January 18, 1903, to participate in the first ever two-way, transatlantic communication, with King Edward VII of England. The plan was to transmit President Roosevelt's message to a station in Glace Bay, Nova Scotia, and then on to Poldhu, England. They would then wait for a reply in the reverse order.

The president's message was tapped out in Morse code, but instead of getting confirmation from the Canadian station that the message had been sent on to England, they received a pleasant surprise—a response directly from the King. Conditions were so good that evening that the message was picked up in Poldhu and transmitted directly back to Wellfleet, making it the first wireless telegram between America and Europe.

What began as simple transmissions from crude, timber towers in South Wellfleet quickly evolved into North America's primary "ship to shore" wireless communication station. Rising above skeptics and technical, financial, and political problems, Guglielmo

Marconi gave the world radio and went on to win the 1909 Nobel Prize for his contribution. This technology has since become a radical scientific and social phenomenon, changing the face of the earth's economy and cultures.

THE LONG-AWAITED CANAL

- 1914 -

When the Pilgrims first settled in Plymouth in 1621, the need for a passage across the neck of the Cape was apparent. Myles Standish and William Bradford were among the early explorers who discovered that the Manomet River drained into Buzzards Bay in the west, and the Scusset River, a short distance overland, drained toward the east into Cape Cod Bay. It was Standish and Bradford who set the idea in motion to somehow connect the two tidal rivers, thus connecting two bays.

As early as 1676, the General Court of Massachusetts formally spoke of building a canal through Barnstable, but little did they know this project would remain on the drawing board for 200 years. A century later, at the outbreak of the American Revolution, they were still talking. On June 10, 1776, George Washington inquired with Massachusetts Governor James Bowdoin about the potential of a canal being built to help thwart British offenses in the Cape Cod Bay area. While this inquiry led to the undertaking of the canal's first proper engineering survey, no action was taken.

Throughout the early and mid-nineteenth century, many more surveys were conducted, and engineers gave favorable reports as to the possibility of a waterway being cut, yet none of the proposed projects moved forward. By 1860, the state decided to undertake the task, but the outbreak of the Civil War resulted once again in the postponement of the project. A pressing need for a canal grew, as ships continued to wreck in the dangerous shoals and sandbars when navigating around the outer Cape.

After the Civil War ended and the country began to stabilize, the Legislature of Massachusetts created a special charter, incorporating a company called the Cape Cod Ship Canal Company. It was established on June 26, 1883, and was given until June 26, 1891, to complete what would be the largest canal in the world.

The biggest geographical hurdle was to be found in the extreme difference in tides. The peninsula of the Cape acts as a breaker for the Atlantic Ocean and slows down the arrival of high tide into Cape Cod Bay. Buzzards Bay is less protected, and therefore high waters arrive more than three hours earlier than in Barnstable, and low waters arrive more than four hours sooner. At various times during the day, the water in Barnstable Bay can be 5.79 feet higher or 4.66 feet lower than the water in Buzzards Bay.

Conflicts arose as to whether or not to include locks and whether or not the shallow water would freeze. Debates were held to determine the type of profit that could be expected and the overall practicality of a canal at Cape Cod. Not surprisingly, all the struggles between engineers, scientists, and financers never allowed the project to get off the ground. It wouldn't be until the twentieth century that modern engineering and a wealthy venture capitalist would bring the Pilgrims' vision to fruition.

New York tycoon August Belmont Jr. might be best known for creating Belmont Park, where the prestigious Belmont Races are held. But if racehorses weren't a risky enough endeavor, Belmont spent most of his family fortune investing in two major mass transit projects: the New York City Subway and the Cape Cod Canal.

In 1904, Belmont purchased the Boston, Cape Cod, and New York Canal Company, which held the building charter for the Cape Cod Canal. He hired the prominent civil engineer, William Barclay Parsons, to be the project's chief engineer. Parsons's work on the New York City underground rapid transit system and his consulting role on the Panama Canal made him an ideal candidate to get the job done. On July 29, 1907, construction began.

For two years, a fleet of twenty-six vessels and several crews of men dredged inland from the east and the west, intending to meet in the middle. Work was unexpectedly delayed for three years, as steam shovels were unable to move massive granite boulders formed during the last ice age. Slow progress was unacceptable to Belmont. He was absolutely adamant about his canal opening before the Panama Canal. The three bridges that were built to span the canal—Buzzards Bay Railroad Bridge, and the Bourne and Sagamore vehicular draw-bridges—were all completed by 1912, creating additional pressure to bring the project up to speed. Hardhat divers were sent to shatter the rocks with dynamite, and Parsons brought in extra digging machines, so that in a short time, the project was back on track.

By the spring of 1914, an impressive waterway cut through 7 miles of land, slicing Cape Cod off from the mainland at its shoulder. The Cape was officially an island. The only obstacle separating Buzzards Bay from Cape Cod Bay was a single dam. In celebration of the near-finish, Belmont and Parsons held a ceremony where they bottled the blended waters of the two bays and opened the final sluiceway, or trough.

The Cape Cod Canal officially opened on July 29, 1914—seven years to the day after the start of its construction. A parade of ships, including Belmont's private yacht and the *McDougall* (a US Navy destroyer carrying Franklin Delano Roosevelt, who was Assistant Secretary of the Navy at the time), made their way through the new privately operated toll canal. By establishing a long-term passage between the two bays, Belmont not only completed what so many before him had been unable to do, he achieved his objective of opening the canal seventeen days before the Panama Canal.

What did not live up to expectations was the amount of profit the canal would generate. Tolls were expensive and the passage was narrow, so even if the captain could afford the rates, his boat might not fit in the canal. Even though many mariners continued to use the Atlantic coastal routes and the canal changed hands a few times, the Cape Cod Canal remains the widest sea-level canal in the world, and has become one of the region's most memorable and impressive geographic features.

ASSAULT ON AMERICAN SOIL

~ 1918 ~

Incorporated in 1797, the town of Orleans endured many attacks throughout the country's early wars—until the local militia repelled the British ship *Newcastle* during the War of 1812. More than a century of peaceful existence followed, and then, in the summer of 1918, a German U-boat surfaced and fired on Orleans, making it the only town in the United States directly attacked during World War I.

Although submarine development began in the 1860s, it wasn't until 1895, when Rudolph Diesel introduced an engine to power submarines, that the concept of fighting under the sea became realistic. Submarine technology quickly advanced in the United States and Great Britain, and by the onset of World War I, America, England, France, Germany, and Russia all had submarines.

On Sunday morning, July 21, 1918, the residents of Orleans were going about their business as usual: attending church, fishing, and relaxing. Tourists were idling away the summer in seaside cottages.

The tugboat *Perth Amboy*, with its four barges in tow, was crawling along the Nauset coast at a leisurely pace. Despite the calm normalcy, however, there were a few not-so-subtle reminders that the world was in the middle of a great war. French ships guarded the transatlantic cables that had recently been laid between Orleans and France. An airbase had been built in Chatham, just down the coast from where the Coast Guard diligently patrolled the waters. Nearby shipyards and arms manufacturers were increasing production. The Americans' contribution to the war effort came in the form of ammunition, soldiers, and supplies shipped overseas. Cape Codders were well aware that much of this traffic sailed right past their front doors.

Beginning with the sinking of the *Lusitania* off the coast of Ireland in 1915, the Germans made it very clear that they intended to use their new submarine technology to not only stop the Americans from supplying the Allies but to win the war. The following year, the United States became increasingly aware of the capabilities of the German submarines when several subs made impromptu visits to major East Coast cities, including Baltimore and Newport, under the pretense of doing business. The underlying message: German U-boats could penetrate American waters.

In late 1916, shortly after a German submarine visited Narragansett Bay Naval Station in Newport, Rhode Island, it sailed off into the Atlantic and promptly sank one Dutch and four British ships. It was at this time that the United States began shoring up her coastal defenses. Steel nets were installed across the entrances to major harbors and naval air stations were built to aid in the detection and destruction of enemy submarines.

Not unlike the War of 1812, the United States remained neutral, until it was drawn into the conflict. In 1917, the Germans unleashed their submarine force in unrestricted warfare, and any ship (not just military) found in British waters was considered fair game. In a short period of time, many civilian and merchant ships ended up at the bottom of the ocean. German U-boats attacked American vessels all over the Atlantic and sunk six civilian merchant ships near Nantucket. For Cape Codders, World War I was hitting very close to home.

The United States joined forces with the Western Allies on April 6, 1917. The East Coast remained U-boat-free for a year, but naval commanders knew the enemy might turn toward America at any moment. That time came on June 14, 1918, when a single German submarine, with a crew of seventy-eight, was deployed to American waters.

On its way to lay mines in the New York Harbor, the German U-156 sank one British and two Norwegian ships. On July 19, one of its mines sank a 14,000-ton cruiser, the USS *San Diego,* and before the *San Diego* had even settled to the ocean floor, the U-156 was on its way to wreak havoc along the Cape Cod coast.

On the morning of July 21, 1918, the first shot rang out from the attacking vessel. Onlookers were horrified as the U-156 surfaced and began firing rounds into the *Perth Amboy* and her four barges. A torpedo made a direct hit to the tugboat, setting it ablaze. In all, an estimated 146 rounds were fired into the four boats, and one shell even made it onto the beach!

Uncertain of what was happening, a Coast Guardsman scrambled up the tower of the station to get a better view of Nauset Harbor. Realizing that a German submarine was firing on Orleans, he radioed the naval air station in Chatham and reported that the American mainland was under attack.

As the U-156 continued its assault, other Coast Guardsmen set out in lifeboats to rescue thirty-two people from the burning boats, including the captain, his wife, and his children. The heroes rowed directly into the steady line of fire and eventually brought everyone to safety. Before the U-boat could submerge, HS-2 and R-9 seaplanes from Chatham Naval Air Base arrived, dropping bombs that failed to explode. The Germans slipped away before the navy could launch a more effective counter-attack.

To some extent, the U-boat attack succeeded in frightening the American public, and this one-sided incident was later referred to as the "Battle of Orleans." More enemy submarines followed the U-156 across the Atlantic, sinking more than ninety vessels between Newfoundland and North Carolina, but the Allies' successful anti-submarine campaign quickly brought an end to the menacing German U-boats.

Little tangible evidence of the Battle of Orleans survives today, other than the rusting bits of sunken barges off Nauset Beach and a few frantic telegrams sent between an Orleans resident and the *Boston Globe.* The display of telegrams once hung curiously in the men's room at the Orleans Yacht Club, but is now in the possession of the Orleans Historical Society.

A BRIDGE IS RE-BOURNE

- 1935 -

ONE OF THE MOST IMPORTANT EVENTS IN Bourne's town history is not so much the opening of the Cape Cod Canal but the completion of the Bourne Bridge three years earlier. While the canal was under construction, a railroad bridge and two cantilever drawbridges were concurrently being built—all of which were finished long before there was a canal to cross. On the west side of the Cape, Buzzards Bay Railroad Bridge was completed in 1910 and the Bourne Bridge was finished in 1911, while on the east side, the Sagamore Bridge was finished in 1912.

Privately financed by August Belmont Jr., the Cape Cod Canal was an instant success when it opened on July 29, 1914. The Bourne Bridge accommodated cars and trolleys, with tracks providing service between Monument Beach and New Bedford. Shipping times between the regions north and south of the Cape were improved and tourists began pouring into Cape Cod. The bridges, however, could only be crossed when there was no marine traffic, so automobiles going to and from the Cape experienced many delays—not unlike today!

Boats also experienced delays. The canal had fast currents and winding, narrow passages, and the drawbridges could only open to a width of 140 feet, limiting the size of vessels that could pass through. It only took a few years to realize that the canal wasn't generating the type of revenue that had been projected. Belmont deepened the canal by 5 feet, which increased boat traffic, but it still wasn't as profitable as had been anticipated.

When a German submarine sunk a Cape Cod tugboat off the shore of Nauset on July 21, 1918, the canal became an issue of national security. With little objection from Belmont, the United States government, under Woodrow Wilson's direction, purchased the canal for $11.5 million. In 1928, the Army Corps of Engineers was given the responsibility for the canal and its three bridges, and they maintain it to this day.

While the canal may not have brought huge prosperity to the Cape's upper towns as expected, improvements to the canal and bridges created more than 2,100 jobs during the Great Depression. On September 6, 1933, the Public Works Administration (PWA) authorized the updating and reconstruction of all three bridges. The canal was widened to 500 feet and deepened to 32 feet. The Boston architectural firm of Cram and Ferguson designed the bridges, and Fay, Spofford, and Thorndike of Boston supervised their construction. Whenever possible, they chose to use manual labor instead of machinery.

Foundations for the two new highway bridges were laid in December 1933. The Sagamore Bridge crossed from the mainland of Massachusetts onto the Cape at Sandwich, about 2½ miles from the eastern end of the canal. The Bourne Bridge was constructed just less than 2 miles from the western end. Two years and $40 million later, the canal and bridges were new and improved.

The Bourne and Sagamore Bridges are mirror images of each other. They arch gracefully over the canal and are designed for four lanes of traffic. The elevated bridges provide vessels with a vertical clearance of 135 feet above water and a horizontal clearance of 480 feet.

The two structures differ in that the Bourne Bridge is 2,384 feet long, almost 1,000 feet longer than the Sagamore Bridge. The Bourne Bridge also received critical acclaim prior to opening. It was given the American Institute of Steel Construction's Award of Merit as "The Most Beautiful Bridge Built During 1934," recognizing it as one of the country's most significant and innovative steel bridges of the time.

The Bourne and Sagamore Bridges were dedicated together on June 22, 1935, with lavish ceremonies and aerial shows. A parade consisting of more than 8,000 people crossed over both bridges and marched for 7½ miles along the south side of the canal, entertaining an estimated 200,000 onlookers. Governor James Michael Curley of Massachusetts performed the ribbon cutting at the Bourne Bridge, while Eleanor Robson Belmont, widow of August Belmont Jr. cut the ribbon at the Sagamore Bridge.

Today, more than thirty-five million vehicles a year pass over these two bridges that provide the only land links between Cape Cod and mainland Massachusetts. Several points of interest related to the canal and bridge history are located along the waterway on either side of the canal, but the only part of the original Bourne Bridge that exists is a large concrete wall, which was the old bridge abutment. It is located to the west of the present-day bridge, on the north side of the canal.

THE GRAVEYARD OF THE OCEAN:
THE SINKING OF THE *PENDLETON*
AND *FORT MERCER*

- 1952 -

WE HAVE ALL HEARD OF THE "PERFECT STORM," but have you heard of the "Perfect Wreck"? On February 18, 1952, the SS *Pendleton* was bound for Boston and the *Fort Mercer* was headed for Portland, Maine. These two tankers of nearly identical design, carrying identical cargo, became crippled by identical conditions in the same fierce winter gale. If that isn't similar enough, both tankers broke in half within six hours of each other, at a distance of only 40 miles apart— leaving four halves of two ships bobbing off the coast of Chatham. The parallel calamities of both ships resulted in the greatest Coast Guard rescue of all time.

The *Pendleton* was due to dock in Boston at dawn on February 18, but poor visibility forced Captain John J. Fitzgerald to turn back to sea and wait out the storm. Conditions only worsened, however, and at 5:50 A.M., with no warning other than a few violent lurches, the *Pendleton* split clean in half between its two cargo tanks. The captain and seven officers were stranded in the bow (the front section of the boat), while the other thirty-three engineers and crewmembers were in the stern (the back half of the boat). Fred Brown of Portland, Maine, said the noise was "like the tearing of a large piece of tin . . . a noise that sends shivers up and down the spine and jangles every nerve."

The radio was in the front of the ship, but the engine and power were in the back, so the break severed any chance of contact with the Coast Guard. No SOS signal could be sent. If there was any bright side to being in the rear portion of the ship, it was that the crew could at least steer their half of the boat with the remaining power. The officers up front weren't as lucky. With no electricity in the bow, they were left powerless at the mercy of gale-force winds, heavy snow, and 60-foot waves. As no distress signal was sent, it was not until almost eight hours later that the Chatham Lifeboat Station picked up the *Pendleton* on its radar screen—in two blips rather than one. While the *Pendleton* was being thrashed about less than 6 miles off the coast of Chatham, the *Fort Mercer* was about to suffer the same grim fate 37 miles farther out.

In the wee hours of the morning, the *Fort Mercer* was encountering the same rough conditions. Hours after the *Pendleton* had cracked in two, while its crew was silently suffering in the brutal elements, the *Fort Mercer* was about to lead a somewhat parallel life, but with one distinct difference. The *Fort Mercer* was able to transmit an SOS to the Coast Guard before the ship broke up—their saving grace!

At 8:00 A.M., after hearing a loud crack, Captain Frederick Paetzel immediately alerted the crew and contacted the Coast Guard that an emergency situation was at hand. The Coast Guard alerted their cutters, which were 120 miles away on Nantucket. At 10:30 A.M., the

Fort Mercer was still in one piece, but by noon it was undoubtedly cracked and spurting oil. At 12:03 P.M., the captain issued the final distress call, "Hull splitting," and gave their location at 37 miles east of Chatham. Seven minutes later, the ship broke in two. Similar to the *Pendleton,* nine officers were trapped up front without power and thirty-four crewmen were in the back.

The Coast Guard dispatched five cutters, two lifeboats, and numerous aircraft for the *Fort Mercer,* still unaware of the *Pendleton* disaster. In addition to their luck in having sent the SOS, the *Fort Mercer* was in deeper water, which offered another ray of hope: the waves did not batter it nearly as brutally as the *Pendleton.* However, since the location was farther out, it took a lot longer for the Coast Guard to reach it. The cutters made slow progress, but eventually came upon both pieces of the *Fort Mercer* and began rescue attempts, which lasted well into the next day.

The cutters *Acushnet* and *Eastwind* arrived at the stern of the *Fort Mercer.* Neither ship was suited to draw alongside another vessel, but a few men were recovered by running rubber rafts on lines between the boats. This eventually posed too much of a risk, due to the heaving and rolling of the massive icebreakers, which created roller-coaster-like conditions for those in the rafts. The *Acushnet* managed a daring maneuver by backing in close to the *Fort Mercer* and allowing eighteen men to jump to safety. Thirteen others remained behind due to age, injuries, and the need for expertise to continue steering the half-ship.

As rescue efforts continued at the stern, the Coast Guard cutter *Yakutat* arrived at the bow section of the *Fort Mercer.* They arrived around 6:00 P.M., but spent most of the night unsuccessfully trying to put a transfer line aboard the bow. Knowing they could not be rescued from the bridge, the crew of the *Fort Mercer* devised a plan to tie flags together and lower themselves onto a more protected area of the ship, where there were greater possibilities of rescue. More than twenty hours after the *Fort Mercer* had been ripped in half, a last ditch effort was made to rescue the four remaining survivors, amid thirty-five-foot swells and fifty-knot winds.

A lifeboat and rubber rafts were launched under extremely adverse and dangerous conditions. Due to the captain's ailments, the crew wanted him to go first, despite his insistence on staying with the ship. He jumped, and was plucked from the waves after floundering for about a minute in the icy water. The final three men were taken aboard the rafts, twenty minutes before the bow capsized! By 9:00 A.M. on February 19, four of the nine officers were saved from the bow of the *Fort Mercer*, which was, unfortunately, four more than were rescued from the *Pendleton*.

Sometime during this sequence of rescue operations, a Coast Guard aircraft was searching for *Fort Mercer*'s lifeboats and issued a report that he had spotted the bow of a ship, rolling in the surf off the coast of Chatham. How could this be? Rescuers were already on the scene, no less than 1,000 yards away from the bow of the *Fort Mercer*, but there was no aircraft in sight. The pilot was asked his position, which turned out to be 50 miles away! He flew in to get a closer look and read the name on the bow. This was the first sighting of the *Pendleton*. Well, at least half of it.

The lifeboat captain was in disbelief as was the rest of the Coast Guard. They were dealing with two shipwrecks of the same magnitude, and they already had their hands full with one. Radar operators at the Chatham Lifeboat Station now had the bow of the *Pendleton* in sight. They knew the second unidentified bleep on the radar had to be its stern and recognized that it was drifting rapidly to the south, directly for the Chatham Bar—where it would be in danger of capsizing and being dashed to pieces.

One of the rescue cutters diverted to the *Pendleton* could not get close enough to make a rescue attempt because of the shoals. The men on board could only watch as the lone survivor jumped into the sea, too soon to be rescued. By the time smaller lifeboats could get to the bow of the *Pendleton,* the ravaging storm had claimed the lives of all eight who had been in this part of the boat.

A rescue operation was now underway for the back half of the *Pendleton,* which was being monitored by radar. Chief Engineer Raymond L. Sybert had been steering the stern of the *Pendleton* using an emergency rudder control and was trying not to run aground on the outer Cape. The crew had a portable radio and listened to reports of the *Fort Mercer* rescue, but they weren't sure the Coast Guard was aware of their own dire straits. Hope was renewed when they learned a lifeboat had been sent from Chatham Lifeboat Station—for them!

Four men, in a 36-foot wooden lifeboat with a ninety-horsepower engine, crossed the notorious Chatham Bar into conditions now often compared to the "Perfect Storm." Moving mountains of water shattered the windows, wrenched the compass from its mount, and drove the men over 60- and 70-foot waves into a black hole. Potentially facing their own deaths, these men went bravely forward with selfless heroism—and without a compass.

The boat was navigated with little more than dead reckoning and a good ear through monstrous seas to the *Pendleton*'s stern. The lifeboat captain could see nothing, but he could hear the creaking of the hull and the sounds of metal being pounded by waves. Those stranded on the *Pendleton* clung to hope and watched, spellbound, as the light of the little lifeboat drew closer and closer. Aircraft circled overhead and flares lit the violent scene, as each man climbed one-by-one down a rope ladder to the rescue boat. One man was lost in the waves, but at the end of the day, thirty-two of the thirty-three stern survivors had been rescued. For their heroism, the four crew-men of the lifeboat were later awarded the Coast Guard's Gold Life-saving Medal, comparable to the Congressional Medal of Honor.

Amid hurricane-force winds, 60-foot waves, and snow squalls, and often in pitch blackness, thirty-two of the forty-one crewmem-bers were rescued from the *Pendleton,* and thirty-eight of forty-three crewmember were rescued from the *Fort Mercer,* by a heroic group of men who were at first unknowingly dealing with the uncanny paral-lels of two split tankers. These extraordinary feats of seamanship have gone down as some of the most heroic rescues in the 214-year history of the United States Coast Guard. In all, five gold life-saving medals, four silver life-saving medals, and fifteen commendation medals were awarded—for a total of twenty-four citations for heroism during the two rescues.

The stern of the *Pendleton* rests off Chatham Bar, as a headstone for the graveyard of the ocean. It is a haunting reminder of the old Coast Guard saying: "You have to go out, but you don't have to come back."

GHOST SHIP RISING

- 1985 -

ON THE NIGHT OF APRIL 16, 1717, one of the worst storms ever to hit Cape Cod sank the infamous pirate ship of "Black Sam" Bellamy. The violent wreck sent 144 of 146 men aboard the *Whydah* to their watery graves, just 500 feet from the coast of Wellfleet. Romantic tales of Black Sam trying to reach his sweetheart, Maria Hallett, and stories of the gold and silver plundered from European ships throughout the Caribbean were passed down from century to century.

After a few documented attempts at recovering the booty, nothing more than a handful of gold coins had turned up, and there was no certainty that they had come from the *Whydah*. As time passed, few believed the stories were true and even fewer believed in the existence of this sunken treasure. Luckily, that few included a very persistent and passionate Barry Clifford.

A childhood filled with tales of pirates, a relentless belief in the existence of the *Whydah* treasure, and years of research (along with a little nudging from Walter Cronkite) turned Clifford the salvage diver into Clifford the explorer—but his boyhood dream of finding sunken treasure was a long shot. First, this area along Cape Cod had one of the highest concentrations of shipwrecks on the East Coast, and nothing definitive had ever confirmed the *Whydah*'s exact resting place. Second, there was a general disdain among academic archaeologists toward private archaeological adventures. It wasn't without a lot of arm-twisting, legal wrangling, and penny-pinching that Team Whydah got underway in the early months of 1983.

After rallying private investors, Clifford pulled together a crew, which consisted of friends, fishermen, and fellow salvage divers. Even John F. Kennedy Jr. came along that first summer. The boat, appropriately named *Vast Explorer,* was modified for underwater exploration. It made its maiden voyage from a boatyard in Maine down to Wellfleet, where it began its new life as a research vessel. The expedition muddled through its first season to no avail; the treasure hunters had nothing to show for all their hard work.

The next few years, however, were very different. Beginning July 20, 1984, out of the quicksand of the Atlantic Ocean came cannons, gold bars, and hoards of gold and silver ingots and coins—and they just kept coming. The typical day yielded artifact upon artifact: spoons, kettles, games, medical instruments, and weaponry. More than 6,000 gold coins and bars were recovered and put into a vault, while thousands of other items were conserved or stored.

Items of a personal nature—such as buttons, clothing, jewelry, and even human bones—endowed the long-gone crew with a certain sense of humanity. These items helped piece together what eighteenth-century life aboard a pirate ship had been like, and they helped it become clear that these lives had been lost in a violent manner during a horrific storm.

Clifford was certain he had discovered "Black Sam" Bellamy's ship. It was in the correct location, no other wrecks in the area were said to have carried such a treasure, and there was no record of the booty having ever been recovered. Although Clifford and his crew uncovered nearly 20,000 objects, the Massachusetts Board of Underwater Archaeological Resources refused to recognize the finds as coming specifically from the *Whydah*.

The team knew exactly what it would take. They had to find something marked with the name of the ship, so there would be no doubt. The ship's quarterboard or the bell would do the trick, but did either still exist? The 1985 season was coming to a close. Winter would settle into Cape Cod very soon and money was in short supply. Little did they know that within a few weeks, everything would change.

In early October, the team made their final efforts to check out a large mass that had shown up on the magnetometer (an instrument used to find magnetic objects). One of the divers excitedly commented that there was something huge down there; he believed it to be a bell located very close to where they had found the first group of cannons.

Not wanting to get his hopes up, Clifford went down to have a look. Sure enough, it was a bell, but it was "concreted," or petrified, with layers of salt, making the inscription illegible. At that point, it was impossible to tell which ship the bell belonged to, so emotions were kept in check. With the amount of wrecks in the area, the bell could have been from any number of ships, but the logical assumption was that the heaviest items, such as cannons and bells, sank quickly, never far from where the ship went down.

On October 7, 1985, the unidentified bell was hoisted from the water and taken to a lab, where it was submerged in a tank of fresh water with an electrical current added. In time, the current broke down the salts, and a lump of the concrete crumbled away, exposing the word "Gally." It was determined to be a different spelling of the modern word "galley," which was a lightweight ship with a big cargo space—the favorite among pirates, but still there was no name. Conservators patiently picked away at the rest of the concrete. After twenty minutes a big chunk fell away, revealing at last the name of their ship:

THE+WHYDAH+GALLY+1716

From that moment on, there was no question as to what Barry Clifford and his team of explorers had found: "Black Sam" Bellamy's ship, the *Whydah,* and the Pirate Prince's sunken treasure.

This is really just the beginning of the story. The *Whydah* is the world's first pirate ship ever excavated, and its booty, estimated by some to be between $20 and $40 million, is the only pirate's treasure ever found. It's not surprising that this small, privately funded venture became an overnight corporation—bureaucracy, lawsuits, and all.

The expedition and conservation is ongoing. Among the 200,000 artifacts now found are extraordinary objects, such as the world's oldest, reliably dated collection of Akan (West African) gold jewelry. In 1998, the hull of the ship was found. The amazing story of this legendary pirate and the man who brought him back to life is told through a fascinating series of exhibits in the privately funded Whydah Museum in Provincetown.

ON THE MOVE: THE HIGHLAND LIGHT

- 1996 -

FOR EIGHTEEN DAYS IN JUNE 1996, a piece of history was not being made, but being moved. The 404-ton Highland Light, now known as the Cape Cod Light, was meticulously raised from its foundations and slowly rolled to a new position, away from the eroding cliff. Cape Cod's first lighthouse no longer saves lives; it serves as a beacon for tourists and photographers rather than sailors.

More than a thousand ships have sunk between Truro and Wellfleet, earning this section of Cape Cod the ominous nickname, "Graveyard of the Atlantic." The worst of it, however, lies about a mile northeast of present-day Truro, near the bend in the "wrist" of the Cape. In 1794, when Reverend James Freeman petitioned Congress for a lighthouse, the shifting sands of Peaked Hill Bar were considered one of the most perilous stretches of coast in the country. According to both Freeman and the Boston Marine Society, more ships wrecked off Truro's eastern shore than in any other part of Cape Cod.

A lighthouse was of dire necessity, and there was no better place for it than the highlands of North Truro. Rolling dunes, reminiscent of northern Scotland, terminated in towering 125-foot cliffs overlooking the Atlantic Ocean. The hillside was made of compacted clay deposits that most believed could withstand the hammering of the waves.

This plea struck a chord with Congress, and in 1796, President George Washington commissioned the first lighthouse to be built on Cape Cod—the twentieth in the United States. The following year, ten acres of land were purchased from Isaac Small of Truro for $110. A 45-foot wooden lighthouse was constructed 500 feet from the edge of the bluff, and Small was appointed the keeper of Cape Cod's first lighthouse, Highland Light.

The powerful lantern, which sat 160 feet above sea level, contained twenty-four lamps and reflectors and was fueled by whale oil. Fearing this light might be confused with the Boston Light, a rotating eclipser was installed to make it appear to flash when viewed from a ship. Although it was on a very slow, eight-minute rotation, the Highland Light became the country's first lighthouse to have a flashing light.

It wasn't long before both the eclipser and the lighthouse keeper were replaced. In 1811, the lantern was updated with a new Winslow Lewis system, and, after complaining that the newfangled lamps required too much work, keeper Small was replaced with a seventy-year-old—who would last only five years.

It is not surprising that, by 1828, the thirty-year-old wooden lighthouse had taken a beating by Mother Nature and was in "very imperfect" condition. Winds often rattled the wooden structure, and the glass lanterns repeatedly broke. In 1831, after being deemed unsafe, the lighthouse was rebuilt in brick. Shortly afterward, a new lantern, staircase, and windows were installed, but according to then lighthouse keeper, Jesse Holbrook, the tower had been hastily constructed, without regard to proper mortar and bond.

No matter how poorly constructed it might have been, the new brick lighthouse served its purpose better than the original wooden one. The keepers made do until 1857, at which time the importance of this light could not be ignored. Ship after ship continued to be lost in the treacherous waters near Truro, prompting another facelift to the tower and the replacement of the reflector system with a new, high-tech Fresnel lens, direct from Paris. Highland Light was now one of the East Coast's most powerful and vital lighthouses.

The issuance of a coal-burning fog signal, powerful enough to cut through the shore's frequent and murky haze, attested to the importance of this station. The keeper was also given two assistants, and his house was once again updated in brick. At the turn of the century, Highland Light was often, quite literally, the first glimpse of America seen by European immigrants. In 1904, an important naval radio station was implemented, and during World War I, Marines guarded the lighthouse.

The Highland Light was electrified in 1932, making its four-million candlepower lantern the coast's most powerful. It was supposedly visible from as far as 45 miles out in stormy weather and could be seen as far as 75 miles away when the weather was clear. Highland Light was automated in 1986, but the house remained in use as Coast Guard lodging rather than a light keeper's dwelling.

When the original lighthouse was built in 1797, it was situated 500 feet from the cliff's edge. In 1856, Henry David Thoreau documented the loss of 40 feet in one year alone, and another 40 feet slipped away in one winter storm in 1990. By the mid-1990s, the steep, clay bluffs had experienced such significant erosion that the lighthouse was only 100 feet away from crumbling into the Atlantic. Today, less than four of the original ten acres that were purchased from Small exist. Highland Light, originally in the business of saving lives, now needed rescuing of its own.

The Truro Historical Society undertook the monumental task of moving Highland Light to a safer position. Its "Save the Light" committee raised more than $150,000, which was combined with $1.5 million in federal and state funds, to pay for the move of the light and the keeper's house. In June 1996, the three-week project was underway.

For several days the foundation of the tower was dug out, and four levels of beams were inserted under the lighthouse in a crisscross fashion. Hydraulic jacks then lifted the entire structure onto rollers, which in turn were set on rails. Thousands of onlookers watched as the 66-foot lighthouse inched its way inland. Coins, which were laid on the beams and flattened as the lighthouse rolled over them, were subsequently auctioned off, with the proceeds going to the Truro Historical Society.

During the move, Highland Light was not as well behaved as it could have been, but eighteen days later it successfully arrived at its new home, 450 feet away from the eroding cliff. It currently stands near the seventh fairway of the Highland Golf Links, where the worst danger is no longer Mother Nature but errant golf balls!

The Highland Light was inaugurated in its new locale on Sunday, November 3, 1996, with guided tours, a relighting ceremony, and the Highland Light Bagpipe Band performing in full regalia. It is currently the country's fourth most powerful lighthouse and remains a functioning Coast Guard light. While the official name was changed to Cape Cod Light in 1976, and maritime charts refer to it as such, to most Cape Codders it will forever be Highland Light.

CAPE COD FACTS & TRIVIA

It is theorized that Icelandic Vikings might have been the first visitors to Cape Cod around A.D. 1004. The thirteenth-century Norse Saga titled the *Flateyjarbok* (Flat Isand Book) gives vivid descriptions of Leif Ericson's journeys across the Atlantic to an area he named "vinland." Some historians believe this to be somewhere along the Cape Cod coast, but archaeological evidence is lacking.

The first recorded European shipwreck off America's east coast happened December 12, 1626. The pilgrim's small boat, *Sparrowhawk,* was grounded in a storm off Nauset Beach after which the governor of the Massachusetts Bay Colony reported this to London.

One of the oldest structures on Cape Cod is the Judah Baker Windmill, constructed in 1791. The Mill began life in South Dennis and was subsequently moved to Kelley's Pond in Dennis before coming to its current resting place in 1866 on River Street in South Yarmouth.

In 1847, Nantucket resident and amateur astronomer Maria Mitchell made the first documented sighting of a comet. This discovery led to her being the first woman elected to the American Academy of Arts and Sciences and the first admitted to the Association for the Advancement of Science.

Brewster bred more deepwater ship captains per capita than all other nineteenth-century American towns.

Thornton Waldo Burgess was born in Sandwich on January 14, 1874. This naturalist and conservationist drew inspiration from his Cape Cod surroundings to create the beloved characters of his Peter Rabbit stories. The Green Briar Nature Center & Jam Kitchen is adjacent to the famed briar patch.

Wellfleet seadog, Lorenzo Dow Baker, was the first to import bananas to the United States and established the United Fruit Company (now, Chiquita Brands International) in 1881.

In 1899, Charles Hawthorne established the Cape Cod School of Art in Provincetown, the first American school dedicated solely to Impressionist painting.

The Provincetown Art Colony (also established by Hawthorne) has been the refuge of artists since 1914, making it the longest continuously running art colony in the country.

Henry Beston's famous book, *The Outermost House,* published in 1928, gives a nostalgic account of a year this naturalist lived in a cottage on the Great Dune of Eastham. His writings helped bring about the creation of the Cape Cod National Seashore and influenced two generations of ecologists, biologists, and conservationists, including *Silent Spring* author Rachel Carson.

Wellfleet resident Luther Crowell invented the square-bottom paper bag in 1872.

Harry Hibbard Kemp (1883–1960), the bohemian Tramp Poet and actor, was a prolific writer who lived his later life out in a shanty on the Provincetown dunes and came to be known as "The Poet of the Dunes."

President Grover Cleveland summered in Bourne at his residence named Gray Gables, which burned down in the 1970s.

The Cape Cod Pilgrim Memorial monument is designed after the Torre del Mangia in Siena, Italy, and was constructed by the U.S. Army Corps of Engineers. The campanile style tower stands 252 feet high, making it the tallest all-granite structure in the United States. It was funded by descendents of the pilgrims and President Theodore Roosevelt spoke at the laying of the cornerstone, August 20, 1907.

The steeple of Wellfleet's First Congregational Church is the only town clock in the world that keeps ship's time.

The Woods Hole Oceanographic Institution (WHOI), founded in 1930, is a research facility dedicated to all aspects of marine science. It is located just south of the town of Falmouth and is the largest independent oceanographic institute in the world.

On July 25, 1956, two ocean liners traveling at full speed through thick fog collided into each other just south of Nantucket. The luxury Italian liner *Andrea Doria* was struck by the Swedish ship, *Stockholm* and sunk in 225 feet of treacherous water, taking 51 lives with it.

The Kennedy family sweated out the 1960 election in Hyannisport. After learning he was elected thirty-fifth president of the United States, John F. Kennedy gave a short speech at the National Guard Armory in Hyannis, putting Cape Cod in the international spotlight for years to come.

Recognizing the need to preserve the Cape's natural beauty, John F. Kennedy signed legislation to create the Cape Cod National Seashore on August 7, 1961.

The Wampanoag Tribe of Gay Head (Aquinnah) on Martha's Vineyard became a federally acknowledged tribe in 1987 through an act of Congress. Its Tribal Lands include Gay Head Cliffs, Herring Creek, Lobsterville, and parts of Christiantown and Chappaquiddick.

In 1945, a young woman of color, Eugenia Fortes, and her friend were asked by the police to leave East Beach in Hyannisport. She refused and later became a civil rights activist and founded the Cape Cod chapter of the NAACP in 1961. On August 28, 2004, the beach she refused to leave was renamed Fortes Beach.

Wellfleet was originally named Grampus Bay due to the large number of pilot whales, also known as grampus or blackfish, that have been stranding themselves along the shores of Cape Cod Bay for centuries.

BIBLIOGRAPHY & SOURCES

Anderson, Robert Charles. *The Great Migration Begins: Immigrants to New England 1620–1633.* 3 vols. Boston: New England Historic Genealogical Society, 1995.

Axtell, James. *The Invasion Within: The Contest of Cultures in Colonial North America.* New York: Oxford University Press, 1985.

Barlow, Raymond E. and Joan E. Kaiser. *The Glass Industry in Sandwich, Vol. 1.* Atglen, Pa.: Schiffer Publishing, Ltd., 1993.

Bradford, William. *Of Plymouth Plantation.* Edited by Samuel Eliot Morison. New York: Alfred A. Knopf, 1989.

Bragdon, Kathleen J. *Native People of Southern New England, 1500–1600.* Norman, Okla.: University of Oklahoma Press, 1996.

Champlain, Samuel de. *Voyages of Samuel de Champlain, 1604–1618.* W. L. Grant, editor. New York: Barnes & Noble, 1967.

Claflin, James. *Lighthouses and Life Saving Along the Massachusetts Coast.* Charleston, S.C.: Arcadia Publishing, 1998.

Clifford, Barry and Perry, Paul. *Black Ship: The Quest to Recover an English Pirate Ship and Its Lost Treasure.* London: Headline Book Publishing Limited, 1999.

Clifford, Barry and Paul Perry. *Expedition Whydah: The Story of the World's First Excavation of a Pirate Treasure Ship and the Man Who Found Her.* New York: Harper Collins, 2000.

Conway, Jack. *Head Above Water: Building the Cape Cod Canal.* Baltimore: Publish America, 2005.

Farson, Robert H. *Twelve Men Down: Massachusetts Sea Rescues.* Yarmouth Port, Mass.: Cape Cod Historical Publications, 2000.

Hathaway, Charles B. *From Highland to Hammerhead: The Coast Guard and Cape Cod.* Chatham, Mass.: By the author, 2000.

Heath, Dwight B., ed. *Mourt's Relation: A Journal of the Pilgrims at Plymouth.* Cambridge, Mass.: Applewood Books, 1986.

Johnson, Robert Erwin. *Guardians of the Sea: History of the United States Coast Guard, 1915 to the Present.* Annapolis, Md.: Naval Institute Press, 1987.

Kupperman, Karin Ordahl. *Settling with the Indians: The Meeting of English and Indian Cultures in America, 1580–1640.* Totowa, N.J.: Rowman & Littlefield, 1980.

Lombard, Percival Hall. *The Aptucxet Trading Post: The First Trading Post of the Plymouth Colony.* Bourne, Mass.: Bourne Historical Society, 1968.

Peters, Russell. *The Wampanoags of Mashpee.* W. Barnstable, Mass.: Indian Spiritual and Cultural Training Council, 1987.

Pletcher, Larry B. *It Happened in Massachusetts.* Guilford, Conn.: Globe Pequot Press, 1999.

Schneider, Paul. *The Enduring Shore: A History of Cape Cod, Martha's Vineyard, and Nantucket.* New York: Henry Holt & Company, Inc., 2001.

Sheedy, Jack. *Cape Cod Companion: The History and Mystery of Old Cape Cod.* Barnstable, Mass.: Harvest Home Books, 1999.

Winslow, Edward. *Good Newes from New England.* Bedford, Mass.: Applewood Books, 1996. First publication in 1624.

Wood, William. *New England's Prospect.* Amherst, Mass.: University of Massachusetts Press, 1977.

Web sites
www.BarnstablePatriot.com
www.BourneHistoricalSoc.org
www.bbc.co.uk/Suffolk
www.CapeCodHistory.us
www.CapeCodOnline.com
www.CapeCodProvisions.com
www.ccmnh.org (Cape Cod Museum of Natural History))
www.EarlyAmerica.com
www.EasthamHistorical.org
www.FalmouthHistoricalSociety.org
www.HistoricNewEngland.org
www.HistoryMatters.gmu.edu
www.MassMoments.org
www.MayflowerHistory.com
www.mwdc.org (MetroWest Dive Club)
www.nha.org (Nantucket Historical Association)
www.OceanSpray.com
www.PBS.org
www.PilgrimHall.org
www.SandwichCapeCod.com
www.SandwichGlassMuseum.org
www.town.brewster.ma.us
www.uscg.mil (United States Coast Guard)
www.USCranberries.com

INDEX

ABOUT THE AUTHOR

Shawnie Kelley is a full-time writer living in Columbus, Ohio. She and her fiancé, Kevin Foy, are often found gallivanting about the Cape, which they consider their "home away from home." Favorite spots include Sandwich, Chatham, and P'Town. Aside from teaching architecture- and travel-related classes, Shawnie enjoys photography, golf, and cooking—and is very much looking forward to their autumn wedding on the Cape.